Project and Production
SCHEDULING

Project and Production
SCHEDULING

by Quentin W. Fleming,
John W. Bronn, and Gary C. Humphreys

Probus Publishing Company
Chicago, Illinois

This publication is designed to provide accurate and authoritative information in regard to the subject matter covered. It is sold with the understanding that the publisher is not engaged in rendering with the understanding that the publisher is not engaged in rendering legal, accounting or other professional service. If legal advice or other expert assistance is required, the services of a competent professional person should be sought.

FROM A DECLARATION OF PRINCIPLES JOINTLY ADOPTED BY A COMMITTEE OF THE AMERICAN BAR ASSOCIATION AND A COMMITTEE OF PUBLISHERS.

Library of Congress Cataloging in Publication Data

Fleming, Quentin W.
  Project and product scheduling.

  Includes index.
  1. Scheduling (Management) I. Bronn, John W.
II. Humphreys, Gary C. III. Title.
TS157.5.F54 1987   658.5'3   86-21189
ISBN 0-917253-63-9

Library of Congress Catalog Card No. 86-21189

Printed in the United States of America

    3 4 5 6 7 8 9

Contents

Preface

This book was written because it has been many years since a comprehensive textbook or primer on the subject of scheduling has been available to the public. Many advances have been made in the field of scheduling in the decade or so since that publication first appeared.

Dramatic changes in the function of scheduling are now taking place almost monthly. These are not affecting the basic techniques used by the schedulers, but are allowing these people to respond more quickly to the requirements of modern business in a way never before possible.

The industrial world is into its third wave of a magic called computers. As exciting as the computer mainframes of the 1960s, and later the minicomputers of the 1970s, were, the most significant and far reaching changes may well be happening now as a result of the newest kid on the block — the "micro" or "personal computer." Everyone seems to have them, including the schedulers, and they are making good use of them. We are seeing the rebirth of network scheduling. It is truly an exciting time.

These new products have given those people whose job it is to plan and make things happen according to a time plan new opportunities to practice their trade. Tasks that once took hours to do are now being done in a matter of minutes. And, as anyone who has ever prepared a schedule knows only too well, it is the replanning and rescheduling and "what-ifs" that fill the daily routines. The addition of microcomputers and associated software packages have probably done more to add professionalism to the art of scheduling than any other single change.

The next to the last chapter of this book is devoted to the subject of "automated scheduling." No specific hardware products or software packages are emphasized. Rather, the subject is reviewed in a generic way, with special emphasis on those functions which lend themselves to automation, where the developments now stand, and on what changes we may see in the future.

The art of scheduling is becoming more sophisticated with each passing day, as new scheduling software packages, now numbering over 100, are introduced. Some even feel that the art is becoming a science. Perhaps. However, one cannot help but to still be impressed by that vanishing breed of individuals who somehow "instinctively" know the right scheduling approach to use and the exact right time to use it. To these people, scheduling will always be more an art.

This book hopes to contribute to the field of scheduling, to assist both the young scientists and the old artisans who share the common goal of getting the job "done on time."

Quentin W. Fleming
John W. Bronn
Gary C. Humphreys

Acknowledgments

Our special "thank you" extends to seven individuals who took time out of their busy schedules to read the draft of this book and to give us their comments and suggestions prior to publication.

From the United States Government:

ROBERT R. KEMPS, Deputy Director of Project and Facilities Management, Department of Energy, Washington, D. C. 20585.

From private industry:

JESSE CARTER, Manager of Systems Compliance, Lockheed Missiles & Space Company, Inc., Sunnyvale, California; **EDWARD RAWLINSON JR.,** Manager of Division Master Planning and International Production Operations, Northrop Corporation, Aircraft Division, Hawthorne, California; **PETER K. SIMON,** Vice President, Turner International Construction, New York; **HAROLD "KIM" SMITH,** Vice President of Operations, Humphreys & Associates, Newport Beach, California.

From the academic community:

JOHN ADAMS, PhD, Associate Professor, School of Business, Western Carolina University, Cullowhee, North Carolina, and Director for Educational Services for the Project Management Institute (PMI); LINN C. STRUCKENBRUCK, PhD, Associate Professor of Systems Management, Institute of Safety and Systems Management, University of Southern California.

List of Figures

Chapter 1

Why Schedule?

People unconsciously schedule—every day of their lives.

A person accepts a new job starting at 8:00 AM each morning, working Monday through Friday. In order to get to work on time the person must work backwards from 8:00 AM. They must set aside sufficient time from the point they awake, to do all of the things they want to do to prepare themselves for work. A man may like to get up, make a pot of coffee, read the morning paper, shave, shower, start the car, and drive to work. Whatever he chooses to do in preparation for work, he must estimate the time involved and subtract it from the time he plans to be at work, i.e., at 8:00 AM. All this activity is a type of simple personal scheduling.

Those of us who drive the freeways to work each day have the opportunity to observe some interesting scheduling phenomena. Quite often we will see men shaving themselves with one hand and driving their car with the other. Other times we will see a woman putting on her makeup and steering with the other hand. While it may on the surface look like men shaving and women applying makeup, that is not what they are really doing. Rather, they are all sharing a common goal of scheduling themselves to arrive at work—on time. Those things which they had planned to do prior to departing the house somehow did not get done. Now they are trying to recover from a "behind schedule" condition by performing those late tasks concurrent with the drive to the job.

The point is that scheduling is something that we do unconsciously every day. If such is the case, then why should anyone bother to take the time to learn about a subject they know intuitively and use in their daily lives ? The answer lies in the degree of complexity. The personal scheduling that we all do in our normal existence is very basic and simple. We do it automatically without giving it any thought. But should the time come where we get involved in a project of considerable size, with multiple complexities spanning long periods of time, and utilizing considerable resources, our own or someone else's, then it becomes essential that we know something about a subject called *scheduling*. Just what it is, how it is used, and why it is needed when certain challenges come our way suddenly becomes important to us.

■ ■ ■

Before getting too far into the discussion on scheduling, it is time to pause and define a few basic terms that will be used many times in this book. They are simple everyday terms but should be fully understood in the manner in which they will be used in this book.

Definitions of Scheduling Terms:

SCHEDULE—A time plan of goals or targets which serves as the focal point for management actions.

SCHEDULE—"A timetable for performing activities, utilizing resources, or allocating facilities."[1]

[1]"Design of the Scheduling System" by William E. Sandman, appearing in Chase and Aquilano, *Production and Operations Management* (Richard D. Irwin, Inc., Homewood, Illinois, 1981), page 425.

SCHEDULE—"A list of the time certain things are to happen; timetable; a timed plan for a project; a list of details."[2]

SCHEDULING—The act of preparing and/or implementing schedules.

EVENT—Something that happens at a point or moment in time.

MILESTONE—An event of particular importance, i.e., a big event.

ACTIVITY—Something that occurs over time. The subject of the plan; that which must be accomplished. Also referred to as a "task."

SEQUENTIAL—Things that are done in a sequence, serial, or series; one thing after another.

CONCURRENT or PARALLEL—Two or more tasks that are done at the same time or at times which overlap.

DEPENDENCY or CONSTRAINT—Things that cannot happen until something else happens first. Also referred to in scheduling as a "restraint."

Perhaps a few simple illustrations will best "lock" these basic terms into place.

Imagine that it is a Saturday morning and we are finally getting around to washing our car. The act of washing the car is an activity, because its accomplishment happens "over a period of time," say one hour. This activity of car washing will begin with the starting event of "car wash-started," and will end with the event of "car wash-completed." All events by definition happen at a moment or point in time. If it has been a year or more since the car has last been washed the neighbors are likely to want to elevate the event of car washed up to that of a "milestone," because it is an event of particular importance—to the neighborhood.

When you wash your car by yourself everything you do is done in a sequential way, one thing after another. You get the pail out, hose down the car, soap it, rinse it, etc., everything done in sequence. However, if you can "con" the excited

---

[2]Webster's "New World Dictionary," Popular Library, Inc, 1958, appearing in James J. O'Brien, *Scheduling Handbook* (McGraw-Hill Book Company, New York, 1969), page 1.

neighbors into helping you with this long-overdue project, then work can take place in parallel or concurrently. One neighbor can soap the car, while another rinses it, while you go get a beer for yourself.

Now that you're on somewhat of a roll you may want to wait until the car wash job is just completed and then walk out with a can in your hand and say: "Hey guys, look what I just found, a can of car wax, why don't we go ahead and. . . ." If your friends are still interested in upgrading the neighborhood you just might get your car polished as well. But the point of this last activity, that of waxing your car, is that it is sequential, that is, it can only happen after the car has been washed. And since the car cannot be waxed until the car has been washed, the event of start waxing cannot begin until the event of car washed has been completed. Therefore, there is a dependency of one event to another. The wax job, which you had planned all along, was "dependent" or "constrained" or "restrained" on the completion of the wash job.

■ ■ ■

Communications

On a large job which might engage vast numbers of people, one of the big tasks confronting any organization is how to communicate with all persons on the job and to help individuals work together as one team. Industry long ago found that one of the best methods to facilitate communications on a large scale was by way of a formal published schedule. The schedule conveys to all concerned persons what management hopes to have accomplished at certain points in time. As things happen or don't happen according to plan, everyone concerned has a point of reference with which to discuss the subject. Schedules facilitate communications.

Planning

Perhaps more basic than the issue of communication is the fact that a schedule is an essential part of any plan. Try to imagine a plan which lacks a time reference, a commitment to accomplish something by specific dates. In law, a contract must convey a commitment as to time or it may likely fail the test of "certainty" and thus be deemed unenforceable by the courts. Likewise, a plan that is void of a commitment to accomplish results as of points in time would also fail for uncertainty or vagueness. All plans require a time commitment, which is another way to say that all plans must have a schedule in order to be viable.

Management Requirements

Management has certain requirements which can be met only through the use of schedules. For example, management universally insists on knowing how well or poorly things are going on a job, from start to finish, in order to take the necessary corrective actions to stay on its plan. Without a time plan by which to measure performance, there can be no basis for assessing with any degree of certainty just how well or poorly things are being done. No competent management would ever proceed with a project based simply on having "confidence" that things will happen as planned. Management needs and demands assurances that events will take place when expected. The vehicle management normally uses to make an assessment of the time results is the schedule.

The schedule is the device which tells management how long a project should take. Typically a project is subdivided into subordinate tasks, with each of these smaller activities time phased through to completion. With this information in hand an estimate of how much time a given job will take can be made with reasonable certainty. With the understanding of the time duration of a project, and the desire to have something done by a certain point in time, management will then know when they must start a job in order to have it completed at the desired point in time.

Management by Exception

With a formally published and agreed to schedule in place, management can make efficient use of its time by monitoring a particular job on an exception basis, rather than having to review everything in a comprehensive way. Management approves the working plan. The use of a schedule allows a given job to be followed by management by watching only those issues which require management's attention, i.e., those things which may not be happening in accordance with the approved plan. Thus management can make best use of its limited time by focusing exclusively on the departures from the plan. A schedule in place allows management to manage by exception.

■ ■ ■

The Triple Constraint

Before we leave the introduction to scheduling, we would be remiss if we failed to put the subject into its proper perspective in the overall process of management. Scheduling is not an end in itself. It is merely one tool which managements everywhere use to control their destinies. Scheduling is an important aid in the overall process of management.

Of greater significance is the fact that scheduling is one part of that delicate three-dimensional aspect of managerial performance which some people have chosen to call the "Triple Constraint."[3]

[3]Milton D. Rosenau, Jr., *Successful Project Management* (Belmont, California: Lifelong Learning Publications, 1981), page 4.

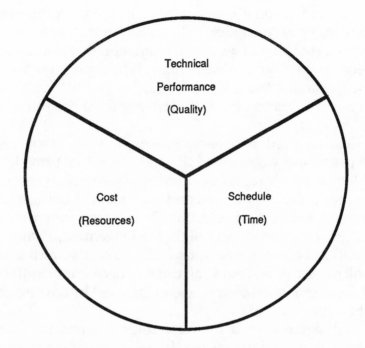

**FIGURE 1-1 THE THREE DIMENSIONS OF JOB/PROJECT
PERFORMANCE**

In very simple terms the concept of Triple Constraint views all projects or jobs as having three performance dimensions (cost/schedule/technical), as is shown in Figure 1-1. All three dimensions must be satisfied and must stay in relative balance with each other in order to successfully complete a given job.

At the top of this three-dimensional diagram is shown technical performance. Technical performance is paramount to everything that happens. It is of primary interest to the buying customer, whether it be the construction of a nuclear reactor, the design of an airplane, providing some type of training, or whatever. It is the principal thing that one has contracted to provide, a service or a deliverable product. If technical performance is not given in the same terms as that originally conceived in an agreement, one will end up with an unhappy customer.

Inherent in the dimension of technical performance is the idea of acceptable quality. When one contracts for something one has a standard of quality in mind, and that standard unless otherwise specified is always high. When one buys something one expects that thing to work. Quality is not a fourth dimension to performance, but is an innate part of the primary technical job.

Cost as used here is synonymous with resources, and resources are always limited. It is resources that provide people and the necessary capital equipment to perform on any job. Our economic system is devised on the concept of doing a job with something left over called profit. Of the three dimensions cited, management, particularly higher management, is most sensitive and will give their closest scrutiny to cost performance. But, as will be discussed below, all three dimensions are interrelated and the degradation of one is soon followed by adverse changes in the other two.

Last but not least in these three dimensions is that of scheduling. Scheduling is the "time" element of performance. Time performance can represent either the completion of a total job by a certain date (a one-time-only project), or it can also indicate that a certain rate of production will be achieved as of a specific point in time, e.g., that say 200 units of something will be produced each month (a recurring job).

When a company opens a new manufacturing plant it automatically gets involved in the "Triple Constraint" of performance, whether it is aware of it or not.

The first task facing the new plant is to prove that it can produce the articles it opened its doors to produce—period. It must build the things it planned to build, including the desired level of quality. As was said earlier, quality must be an integral part of technical performance. It is not acceptable to produce something that does not work or does not work to the levels expected by those consuming the product. Poor workmanship does not satisfy the dimension of technical performance.

Normally the next step a new plant will take is to prove that it can produce the manufactured articles to meet the time dimension, to produce them at the desired rate of production. While meeting the time element the technical/quality standard previously achieved must be maintained. It would not be acceptable to reach a desired rate of production, but with a degraded technical or quality level. A consistent relationship must be maintained.

After the articles have been produced meeting the desired levels of technical/quality, and within the planned production rate each period, the last step is to meet the cost targets. Can these items be made at a cost which allows a profit for the investors?

Although this illustration has been intentionally simplistic, its purpose was to attempt to point out the interrelationship of the three dimensions of the Triple Constraint: technical, cost, and schedule. After having been established, the three dimensions must maintain their relative positions or an imbalance will occur. Changes cannot occur in one dimension without having an impact on one or both of the other elements.

Delays in the schedule usually mean higher costs. Achieving higher technical/quality standards will result in higher costs, or time/schedule delays, or both. And as certain auto makers once tried to put over on the American public, a reduction in quality standards will allow for lower costs and/or higher profits—but not for long.

The principle that we are attempting to illustrate is that managements around the world are subject to the scrutiny of their performance, and that such performance has three elements: technical (including quality), cost, and schedule. In this book we plan to focus on only one of the three—the time element, which takes the form of a *schedule*.

■ ■ ■

In this book we hope to build a case for the use of schedules in most business settings. Schedules help to complete jobs in the time allotted. They also provide for the efficient management of an enterprise. And, in more sophisticated applications, schedules can be used to determine and allocate the correct application of a firm's scarce resources.

We will cover the issue of planning—deciding what to do before starting out to do it. Planning is considered by many astute managers to be an essential prerequisite to putting a schedule in place. Planning techniques used by the United States Government will also be discussed.

Over the past hundred years or so there has been an evolution of scheduling methods, and we will trace them briefly so as to better understand our present position. Some of the scheduling techniques used today are very simple, as with Gantt and milestone charts, but they do work well in many business applications. Other techniques are more sophisticated, and have great potential applications—in the right setting.

One of the more sophisticated scheduling techniques, and probably the technique with the greatest potential in scheduling, involves the use of networks, of which there are two types. We will devote several chapters to this important subject.

In addition to the application of schedules to "one-time-only" efforts, there are scheduling methods used to time control those types of jobs which happen over and over, called recurring, or production, efforts. There are two chapters on repetitive schedules.

Probably the most exciting and new aspect of scheduling does not relate to scheduling exclusively, but rather to another industry—computers, namely microcomputers. The advances made in the last five years in this technology and related software programs have allowed giant strides to be made in the field of scheduling. We have a chapter devoted to automated scheduling, and where we think it may take us in the future.

Lastly, we will end the book with management's use of scheduling, i.e., the bottom line.

Chapter 2

Planning:
Setting The Proper
Foundation For Scheduling

"Plans are worthless, but planning is everything"
President Dwight D. Eisenhower
November 17, 1957

In 1957 President Eisenhower went before the National Defense Executive Reserve Conference and made the above remarks. Undoubtedly his hyperbole was illustrating his belief that the "process" of planning is perhaps more important than the resulting "plan" itself. If that was what he meant in his speech then few could take issue with it. The mental exercise of deciding what one wants to do *before* starting to do it has saved much redirection and rework over the years. But as our Chief Executive we would expect that even Ike would have wanted something tangible after all the planning had taken place, something that he could have used to measure the results of others in the implementation of their planning. That something is normally called a plan, and most plans contain some references to time, typically called schedules.

Expanding on Ike's support for the planning process, it would seem that before one sets down to schedule it might be a good idea to have some type of plan in mind. Therefore, the process of planning could rightly be considered a prerequisite to the preparation of schedules. Before one prepares schedules one should have previously done some planning on the subject to be time-phased.

Just what is planning? In its simplest form planning is the setting of objectives, the placing of responsibilities for performance, and the decision as to the allocation of resources necessary to accomplish the goal. One author described the process nicely:"...Planning includes the identification of potential courses of action to satisfy an objective and the evaluation of means to implement the alternatives. These anticipatory efforts lead to the selection of a preferred plan."[1]

Let us review a couple of requirements of the Federal Government which force private contractors to plan their projects.

The Work Breakdown Structure (WBS)

Federal procurement agencies are often criticized in the news media for their extravagances in buying, for example, ashtrays for airplanes costing $500 each, etc. But the fact of the matter is that these governmental bodies do a very nice job in the procurement of major complex items, and in requiring that the necessary planning needed to implement projects of massive scale take place. Perhaps it would be beneficial for us to review the technique used by these public agencies, since most of them use a single method to undertake their planning: namely, the use of the Work Breakdown Structure (WBS) concept.

The Department of Defense (DOD) was the first governmental body to formally impose the use of the WBS on all jobs of a certain size. The DOD defines the WBS as "...a product-oriented family tree composed of hardware, services and

[1]James L. Riggs, *Production Systems: Planning, Analysis and Control* (John Wiley & Sons, Inc., New York, 1981), page 22.

data...which completely defines the project/program."[2] Across town in Washington the Department of Energy (DOE) issued a booklet in 1981 which provided their own definition of a WBS:"...a family tree hierarchy of the products requiring work to be performed in accomplishing the end objective. Unlike a genealogical family tree, however, the products on the lower branches are produced earlier in time than those above. Products that result from work efforts may be hardware...services...and data...."[3]

Note the similarities in these two WBS definitions. In fact they are imposing the same planning requirement on their contractors. They require contractors to define the scope of work, identify what tasks need to be done, and assign responsibility to organizations to perform the work, all with use of their standard WBS framework.

Figure 2-1 provides an illustration of a WBS diagram used to plan a DOE project. But whether a project is from the DOD, the DOE, the National Aeronautics and Space Administration (NASA), or from wherever in the Government, the WBS method is conceptually the same; only the products being planned are different. The WBS concept can be applied to any product of any size.

The DOE booklet continues to describe why they use the WBS to facilitate their planning:

> The WBS technique assists management in the planning and budgeting functions by providing a formal structure which identifies all the products and relates all the work effort required to meet the project objective. By breaking the total product and effort into successively smaller entities,

---

[2]Department of Defense, Military Standard 881, *Work Breakdown Structures for Defense Materiel Items*, (Washington, D.C.: April, 1975), page 2.

[3]Department of Energy, DOE/MA-0040, *Work Breakdown Structure Guide*, (Washington, D. C.: October,1981), page 3.

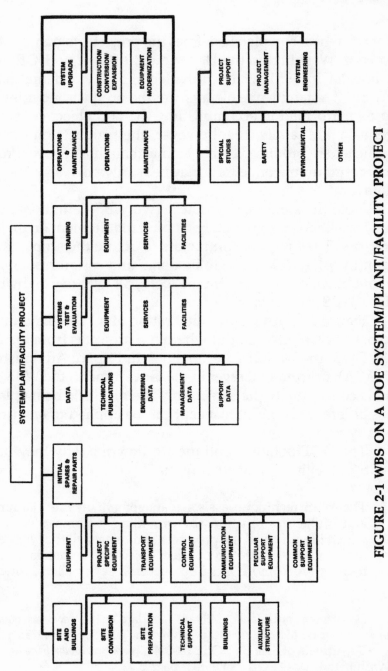

FIGURE 2-1 WBS ON A DOE SYSTEM/PLANT/FACILITY PROJECT
Source: *Work Breakdown Structure Guide*, page A-3.

management can ensure that all required products are identified and addressed.[4]

Let us review the WBS diagram shown in Figure 2-1 to see how it might be used to facilitate the planning. Starting at the top of the WBS is a single box (element) entitled "System/Plant/Facility Project." This is what is referred to as level 1 of the WBS, and at level 1 there is only a single box, since all subordinate/lower tier elements consolidate into the top box, somewhat resembling a pyramid. The WBS diagram may be used to depict an airplane development project, the construction of a shopping center, the building of a destroyer, the construction of a harbor, a new town development, and so forth. In each case the top product that is being developed would be represented by a single box at the top (level 1) of the WBS.

The top box, or more properly, element, at level 1 of the WBS represents the full end item being produced. It is here that the top or master schedule for this project is prepared. The master schedule incorporates a summary of all elements shown at the lower tiers of the WBS, but in broad terms. Intermediate and detail schedules are placed at successively lower levels of the WBS. In a major project there would be schedules prepared for many of the WBS elements, certainly the more critical ones. Schedules for WBS elements at level 5 or 6 would show considerable detail, but must be in concert with the next higher schedules displayed for elements on the next higher level of the WBS, leading up to the top level 1.

The WBS concept facilitates the planning process, particularly on large jobs, by requiring the subdivision of large undertakings into logical and progressively smaller pieces, called WBS elements, which in turn allows each of these elements to be individually planned and managed to a successful completion. Each of these individual elements relates to the next higher element, which in turn relates to the next higher element, all

[4]Ibid, page 17.

of which lead up to the single top element at level 1 of the WBS. Many of these individual WBS elements have their own time reference plan, called a schedule.

The DOE describes the process in their WBS booklet:

> The WBS affords a framework for the aggregation of schedule information by WBS elements to establish overall and detailed schedules. The impact of schedule changes may be readily assessed when a WBS is used because each element's start and completion date is integrated with the other elements' schedules.[5]

Planning is a necessary first step preparatory to making a schedule. The WBS provides an excellent vehicle to take a large and complex project and break it down into smaller pieces, which can then be individually planned, scheduled, and managed. If done properly, the WBS provides the planning framework for the subsequent preparation of a project's schedules.

The WBS is a good technique when used at the proper time, particularly at the start, or better, prior to the start of a new project. It can be used to plan for a large and complex job, or even to lay/out the task of constructing a garage in one's backyard. On large jobs which require the management of millions of dollars in resources, hundreds or thousands of people, and the coordination of multiple organizations and companies, the use of the WBS is ideal.

In any plan there exists an interrelationship between the definition of work to be done, the time phasing of all work/tasks, and the allocation of resources needed to complete a job. This is normally called the budget. Figure 2-2 illustrates the concept of planning a project starting with the preparation of a WBS.

Over the years, since it was first introduced by the DOD in the early 1960s and later formally imposed in 1968, the approach to planning a project starting with the preparation of a WBS has been widely accepted by industry on both public

[5]Ibid, Page 20.

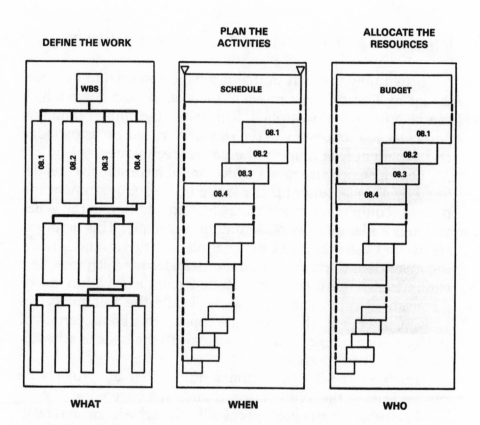

FIGURE 2-2 INTEGRATION OF WORK DEFINITION, SCHEDULING, AND BUDGETING

Source: *Work Breakdown Structure Guide*, page 19.

and private projects. The approach can be used on both large and small jobs. Its utility as a planning aid has been proven and accepted.

Integration & Traceability of Planning and Scheduling

Scheduling is an art in that it must be tailored to fit a particular application. No firm set of rules can be laid down which can be automatically applied. The scheduler must examine a particular job, make a value judgement based on knowledge and experience, and apply the proper techniques.

On those procurements which are of a certain size (as defined by a dollar amount) the United States Government imposes a requirement called "C/SCSC" in addition to the WBS, which is a planning/work definition technique. This acronym stands for Cost/Schedule Control Systems Criteria, and is nothing more than thirty-five criteria or standards which may be a contractual requirement on selected contracts within major government programs or projects. While the full subject of C/SCSC is beyond the intended scope of this book, certain of the thirty-five criteria deal specifically with the issue of scheduling and will be discussed.

The first C/SCSC criterion requires that all projects be planned using the WBS concept, and was covered above.

Two other criteria deal specifically with scheduling and related issues. They are:

I.3 PROVIDE FOR THE INTEGRATION OF THE CONTRACTOR'S PLANNING, SCHEDULING, BUDGETING, ESTIMATING, WORK AUTHORIZATION, AND COST ACCUMULATION SYSTEMS WITH EACH OTHER, THE CWBS AND THE ORGANIZATIONAL STRUCTURE.

II.1 SCHEDULE THE AUTHORIZED WORK IN A MANNER WHICH DESCRIBES THE SEQUENCE OF WORK AND IDENTIFIES THE SIGNIFICANT TASK INTER-

DEPENDENCIES REQUIRED TO MEET THE DEVELOP-
MENT, PRODUCTION, CONSTRUCTION, INSTALLA-
TION, AND DELIVERY REQUIREMENTS OF THE
CONTRACT.[6]

The CWBS mentioned in the first criterion relates to a Contract WBS, which is normally prepared by the contractor and approved by the cognizant Government agency.

To meet these two standards on a large government contract, a private contractor must provide for the integration and traceability of the mentioned activities within its management control system. We will limit ourselves to the scheduling aspects of these requirements.

In effect these criteria require some type of hierarchical relationship between the top master schedule placed at level 1 of the WBS, and those schedules supporting lower level WBS elements down to the lowest element. This requirement is portrayed conceptually in the DOE chart shown in Figure 2-3. From the DOE perspective, their top schedule is reflected in what they call the "Project Master Schedule," which traces down to the contractor's Master Schedule, down through the contractor's intermediate schedules to the bottom schedules, which are described in the chart as a "Work Package." The exact titles of schedules and the terms used will of course vary depending on the particular industry.

A contractor generally satisfies the traceability and integration requirements by preparing what resembles an "organization chart for schedules," typically referred to as a "Schedule Tree." See Figure 2-4 for an example of a contractor's schedule tree. Displayed at the top of the chart is the contractor's master schedule, followed below by intermediate level schedules, which are in turn followed by the detailed lower level schedules. Each box displayed shows the title of the schedule, and it is also useful to indicate the corresponding WBS number.

[6]Department of Energy, DOE/CR-0015, *Cost and Schedule Control Systems Criteria For Contract Performance Measurement-Implementation Guide*, (Washington, D.C.: May,1980), Attachment 2, page 2-1.

On a smaller job one person may handle all of the needed schedules, perhaps as a secondary task to a primary assignment. On a large program, however, it is probably wise to delineate in a formal way precisely who is responsible for the scheduling activity in each of the various functions in a firm. Without a formal structure, with specific individuals charged with the responsibility for the preparation of these documents, schedules may or may not happen. Or, more than likely there will be gaps in the full complement of schedules, and some of the key areas will not be represented with a time plan. It is not critical that a separate scheduling group be established; but it is vital that there be a placement of responsibility for schedules in each major function of a company.

The same group which prepares the master schedule normally takes the lead in defining who is responsible for the scheduling in each function, and for the issuance of procedures to be followed in schedule preparation. To provide some basis on which to communicate, scheduling procedures should specify the recommended display format and symbols to be used, rather than allowing each group to create a new language to display, for example, a simple "start" event. Some people are from the old school, which feels that schedules should enlighten and not confuse the intended audience.

Resource Allocation and Leveling

This is probably the right place to briefly introduce a concept which is gaining in popularity and is becoming an increasingly practical tool with the broadened use of mini and the microcomputers. The subject will be covered in more detail later in the book. The concept is "resource analysis, allocation, and leveling," and the supporters of this approach feel that a schedule should never be approved until resources have been initially allocated to the tasks being scheduled, analyzed, and then leveled to their most efficient use. With more and more projects

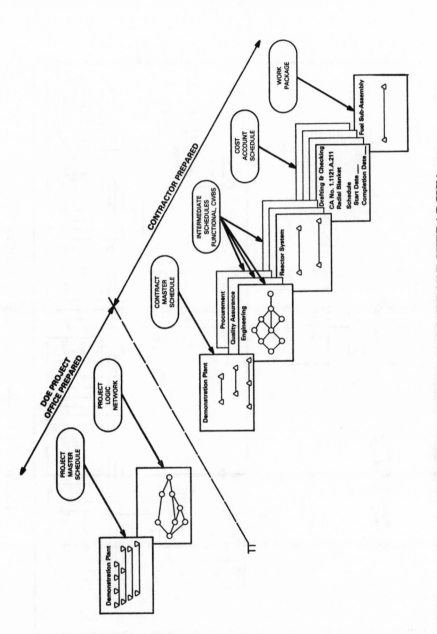

FIGURE 2-3 A TYPICAL SCHEDULE HIERARCHY
Source: *Cost and Schedule Control Systems Criteria*, page 26.

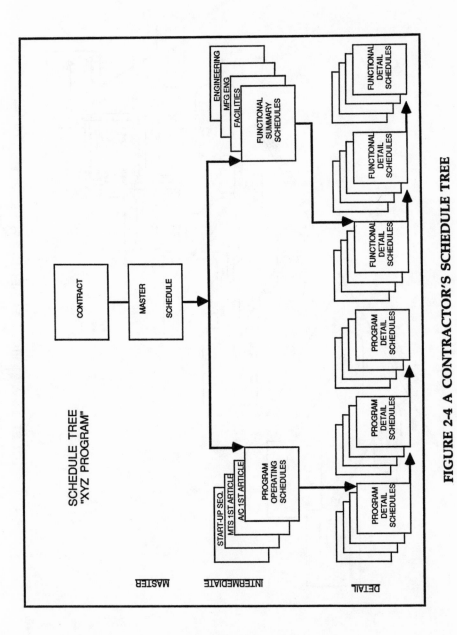

FIGURE 2-4 A CONTRACTOR'S SCHEDULE TREE

being started and then slowed because of funding limitations, the concept is hard to ignore. Both the Government and private industry operates under funding limitations and the concept can be applied nicely.

Resources in the planning phase are fully interchangeable, in that they are represented by money, and money can be used to purchase anything. However, once the plan has started and the resources/funding have been committed to specific objects (cement, civil engineers, trucks, etc.), they are no longer freely interchangeable—-without a severe cost penalty. Therefore, the ideal time for initial resource planning is prior to the go-ahead of work, when everyone starts their respective tasks. However, resource analysis, allocation, and leveling can take place at any time, even after a project begins.

This type of analysis requires a basic decision up front: which is most important to a project, time or money ? With an effort like the Manhattan project, where the United States was trying to develop a big bomb before the enemy, time was obviously the major consideration. If one is building a garage in the backyard out of the current paycheck and future funds, resources become the major issue. Perhaps work can start out of this week's paycheck, but the job can't finish until we get our tax refund back from the IRS!

Once started, most projects are likely to be influenced by time considerations, that is the pressure to get a job done at the earliest possible time. However, as most projects are started with some type of resource constraint, the practice of allowing everyone to start their respective tasks at their own pleasure becomes highly questionable. Critical/high risk tasks should always be started at the earliest possible moment to reduce potential risk areas. But on every job there are activities which can happen now or later which are not critical to the completion of the total job.

Managements responsible for the total job must make an assessment from their perspective as to which tasks they want to happen right away, and which should be delayed till a later time frame.

The "Schedule Baseline"

A wise man once said that there are three certainties in life:
- Taxes
- Death
- *Changes* to Statements of Work

There are multiple uses for schedules. They incorporate plans and add a time reference, which tells one how long it will take to get where one wants to be. After starting on the journey, but prior to arrival, a good schedule should indicate two things: how much progress has been made thus far, and how much longer it will take to get to that final destination.

But what happens if after starting out, someone changes the route, i.e., the Statement of Work changes as that wise man said that it would. If we have not bothered to previously set what some choose to call a "Schedule Baseline," then we have no basis for now predicting with any confidence exactly how long it will take us to get where we want to be via our constantly changing route.

The schedule baseline represents the commitment of an organization to a time goal. Perhaps of greater importance, however, the baseline, if done with broad involvement of all departments, will represent a time commitment from each of the individual managers whose support to the plan is vital to its success. Additionally, the schedule baseline will document the basic assumptions which went into the original plan. These assumptions are necessary for a proper analysis of performance on a continuous basis, and are needed to make a prediction of future trends.

Because of the high likelihood that plans will have to be modified before a job is completed, sound management requires that a reference point or baseline be set. The baseline not only allows for the systematic incorporation of changes, but perhaps more importantly, a schedule baseline permits management to manage its time affairs on an exception basis.

The Five Steps to Planning a Project

A decade ago a fine author and expert on project management provided what he described as the essential steps to the planning of a project.[7] Much of what follows will resemble his treatment, modified to reflect the thrust of this book on scheduling.

The five steps to planning a project are as follows:

Step 1—Define the project by identifying specific tasks and responsibilities.

Step 2—Identify project milestones and key interfaces.

Step 3—Prepare the master schedule(initial) and allocate resources(initial).

Step 4—Prepare the detailed task schedules and resource requirements.

Step 5—Reconcile the detailed task schedules/resource requirements with the master schedule/project funds, and formally issue the master schedule and final budget.

We will cover each of these steps in some detail, placing particular emphasis on the time setting aspect of the planning process.

Step 1 in this process is the definition of *all* project work by the laying out of the tasks to be accomplished. The use of a WBS facilitates this initial process, as was covered in the beginning of this chapter. The use of a standard WBS down to level 2 or 3 is necessary and desirable for prudent management and to comply with the first of the thirty-five C/SCSC criteria. Whether the project being planned is a multi-billion-dollar Government nuclear power generator or simply a few-million-dollar private sector shopping center, the WBS makes

[7]Russell D. Archibald, *Managing High-Technology Programs and Projects*, (New York:John Wiley & Sons, 1976), pages 140-179.

sense as a way of detailing all of the necessary tasks. Each of the planned tasks as represented by the WBS elements should have a specific individual named as being responsible for performance of the task.

Often it is useful in planning to prepare what is called a task/responsibility matrix. Such a matrix will list the WBS elements across the top columns, the names of responsible people with their organizations down the side, and relate the two with an "X" at the intersection between the two. This is a way of relating each WBS element to the specific individual and organization responsible for performance of all tasks. Step 1 has as its objective not only the definition of all work to be done, but also the relating of the tasks to specific people and organizations responsible for performance.

In Step 2 the critical interfaces and major project milestones must be identified. The work contained in each element of the WBS must be examined to determine whether or not there are external forces which could constrain the accomplishment of work contained therein. Not only must relationships between one WBS element and another WBS element of the same project be thought through, but also those relationships which will exist between a given WBS element and some outside (non-project) activity. These interfaces or relationships must be known and specified because such dependencies will often prevent performance of effort in the project's WBS task. It is one thing to control one's own destiny, it's another to have to rely on other tasks in the same project to complete a job, and it is still another to be dependent on an outside force to be able to finish a job.

An example of interfaces within the same project would be the tasks of design and procurement. Procurement is held responsible for buying certain items according to plan but often cannot do so until the design people have prepared and released a procurement specification. The task of buying that something is clearly defined and there has been a specific individual named as responsible, but that person has an interface dependency with the design people which, if their effort is delayed, could have an adverse impact on the in ability to complete the procurement task. This is an example of an interface or relationship existing between WBS elements of the same project.

But there are other interfaces which are external to a given project and these can and often do prevent performance in a timely fashion. Construction projects can be defined nicely with the use of a WBS. However, many of the individual WBS elements are constrained by forces external to the project. Often such dependencies exist with governmental regulatory bodies, whether they be federal (e.g., Environmental Protection Agency), state (e.g., harbor commission), or local (an ornery building inspector). Whatever, these forces which are external to a given project can be absolute constraints on the successful completion of any tasks therein. A new building can be designed, but the project cannot be implemented until approval is given by the city planning commission. The implementation of the construction is on hold, awaiting an interface with an organization outside of its control.

All interfaces must be known and included in order to create a realistic and achievable plan.

Another important part of Step 2 is the description of all project milestones, which by our earlier definition are events (points in time) of particular importance. Project milestones are useful because they help management to pace themselves. Milestones are simple to understand and make useful performance monitoring displays. One does not need special training to determine whether or not a milestone has been accomplished. Either the event happened as planned or it didn't. Milestone displays are also useful in keeping higher management informed as to progress made on a given project.

Step 3 is the preparation and initial or preliminary issuance of the master schedule. A master schedule is, by definition, the highest level schedule for a given project. All other schedules and project plans must conform to the parameters set by the master schedule. If the project milestones established in Step

2 were done thoroughly, then much of the work in preparing a master schedule will have already been accomplished.

The master schedule is the "stand back," broad look at a given project. All major project elements and contract commitments should be called out in the master schedule. There should be a close relationship between the WBS and the master schedule in that most of the major elements of the WBS should be represented in some way in this schedule. Much of the management reporting will be based on the tasks called out in the master schedule.

It is here that the available resources should be reviewed and allocated in broad categories. Both the master schedule and the project budgets should be considered as preliminary until compared against the detailed task examination which will come in the next step.

Step 4 is the preparation of detailed task schedules and resource needs. These schedules will take the tasks and elements of the WBS and prepare a schedule to support them. The importance of these detailed schedules cannot be overemphasized because they will verify whether or not the master schedules and project goals can in fact be met. They should be prepared by those individuals who have been assigned responsibility for performance of each of the individual tasks, and who are in the best position to understand precisely what is involved in the effort. Realistic time spans will be set which heretofore had only been estimated in broad terms. Detailed budgets and resource requirements must be analyzed by individual tasks.

Step 5 is the integration of the detailed task schedules/resource requirements with the overall requirements set by the master schedule and project budget, to determine whether or not there is a fit. More than likely there will be some detailed tasks which will take longer than is compatible with the requirements of the overall project goals. Also, the sum of the detailed budget requests will likely add up to more than is available in project funds. An examination must be made of those tasks which are out of phase with the master project requirements.

This type of exercise will be covered in later chapters when we discuss the subject of critical path methodology.

The relationship of the master schedule to each of the subordinate detailed task schedules can be portrayed nicely by use of a schedule tree, mentioned earlier in this chapter.

■ ■ ■

We have been discussing the value of planning and how a plan is a prerequisite to scheduling, since it would hardly make sense to add the time reference (schedule) if one had no firm direction in mind. All this brings to mind a certain conversation which took place years ago between a young lady named Alice and a certain cat by the name of Cheshire. Alice was visiting Wonderland at the time.

Alice: "Would you tell me, please, which way I ought to go from here?"

Cheshire: "That depends a good deal on where you want to get to."

Alice: "I don't much care where—so long as I get somewhere."

Cheshire: "Then it doesn't matter which way you go."[8]

At this point in her life, and with all due respect to our late President Ike, what Alice needed most—was a plan.

[8]Lewis Carroll, *Alice's Adventures in Wonderland & Through the Looking Glass*, (London: Bramhall House, 1960), page 88.

Chapter 3

The Evolution & Types of Schedules in Use Today

Before discussing the types of schedules currently used by industry, it might be wise if we stepped back and briefly examined the history and evolution of scheduling as we know it today.

Evolution of Scheduling

Prior to World War I scheduling as a methodology wasn't known, or at least wasn't acknowledged. People accomplished their tasks much as we all get to work each morning, using our intuitive personal scheduling systems. Then came World War I and the pressures to get munitions into the hands of our troops—now. Suddenly "time" became the overriding consideration and some type of formal procedure or technique was needed to accomplish scheduling in a more systematic manner.

Henry L. Gantt was working at the Frankford Arsenal in 1917 and he conceived the needed technique which has survived today under his name: the Gantt chart. His approach was simple, easy to understand, and accomplished the desired result: to portray a time plan with a brief picture which anyone could immediately understand. The beauty of the Gantt chart was in its simplicity. It displayed activities (or tasks) as a hollow "bar," drawn over a time frame. To reflect progress the hollow bar representing the plan was filled in to the point where work against the task had been accomplished. Some Gantt charts display a dual set of hollow bars, one to reflect the plan, and the bottom bar used to reflect progress against the plan. Either way the concept is the same. Figure 3-1 displays a simple Gantt chart which reflects three tasks leading to a final task of "Systems Test." More will be said about the Gantt chart below when we get into the discussion of the various types of schedules in use today.

Between the two World Wars the pressure for time performance was relaxed, so the search for and introduction of new and better scheduling methods was slowed. To put things into perspective, the Gantt chart took activities or tasks and displayed them over a time scale. Later, others took events (moments in time) and also displayed them over a time scale. These became known as milestone charts. But neither the Gantt charts nor the milestone charts were able to illustrate the relationships between activities or events, i.e., the fact that often there is an absolute dependency of one event or activity on another activity or event. The second activity cannot start or end until the first activity happens. Along towards the end of the 1920s the concept of Operations Research came into fashion.

The Operations Research people felt that the lack of dependency relationships being displayed on Gantt and milestone charts was a severe shortcoming. They therefore focused their attention on such dependency relationships and started the concept of networks, or more properly logic networks.

A Flow Process Chart is shown in Figure 3-2. In this case the logic or effort moves from top to bottom, whereas most schedules would display the same information from left to right

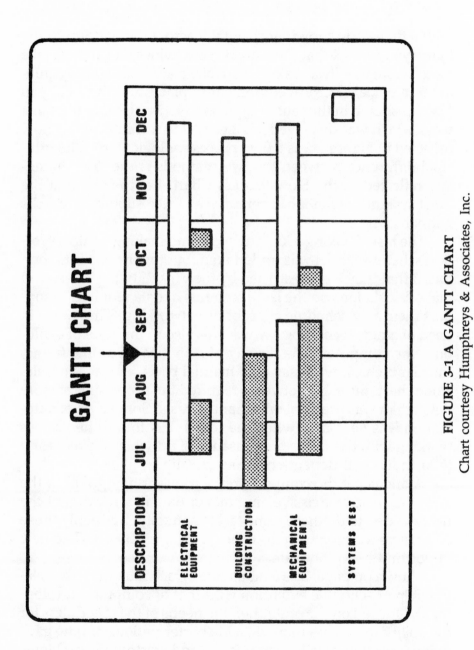

FIGURE 3-1 A GANTT CHART
Chart courtesy Humphreys & Associates, Inc.

with a time scale shown horizontally across the bottom. In the figure you can see that there are three activities which must take place before the "test system" can take place: mechanical equipment in place, electrical equipment in place, and the facility in place as shown in the center sequence. Notice also that the same work which was displayed in Figure 3-1 as a Gantt chart is now reflected in Figure 3-2 as a flow process or logic chart. The principal difference between the two methods is the "dependency" reflected in the Flow Process Chart, i.e.,the fact that the "test system" will not happen until all three subordinate tasks happen first.

The task of taking a logic network and making it into a practical scheduling tool was undertaken, but the proponents soon found that they were restricted by their inability to process and make calculations on the large amounts of data required to support their new schedule concept of networking. They were in need of a new technology which was also in the state of evolution: the computer. The display of activities on a time frame, the Gantt chart, was easy on a manual basis, as was the Milestone chart. But logic networks required the processing of more detail than was practical on a manual basis. Some type of automation was necessary when the schedulers found themselves working with hundreds or thousands of activities or events and their individual dependency relationships.

Along came the computer revolution, bringing with it the ability to process massive amounts of data in a fraction of the time needed to do these same tasks manually. Suddenly those schedulers working with the concept of logic networks had new opportunities to innovate.

Shown on page 42 is a tabulation which illustrates the relationship of schedule evolution with that of computer development. One fed on the other, i.e., the needs of the schedulers for the ability to process more data in shorter periods of time gave to the computer developers practical and worthwhile problems to solve, and solve them they did. And with the introduction of the new computers with their increasingly expanded memory

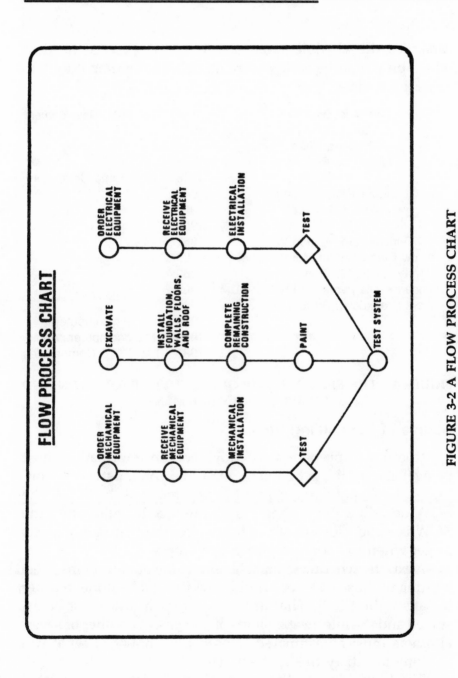

FIGURE 3-2 A FLOW PROCESS CHART
Chart courtesy Humphreys & Associates, Inc.

capacities, the schedulers were able to put into practice the ideas which only months earlier were limited by the time it took to process the data.

Schedule Evolution	Year	Computer Development
Gantt Chart	1917	
Milestone Chart	?	
Operations Research	1928	
	1946	Mainframe Computers
Linear Programming	1947	
Line of Balance	1951	
PERT	1957	
Critical Path Method-CPM	1957	
Arrow Diagramming Method-ADM	1959	
PERT/Cost	1962	
Precedence Diagramming Method-PDM	1962	
Work Breakdown Structures-WBS	1965	
	1970	Minicomputers
	1976	Microcomputers:Apple
	1981	IBM PC & Compatibles

FIGURE 3-3 THE RELATIONSHIP OF SCHEDULE EVOLUTION AND COMPUTER DEVELOPMENT

Source of Scheduling Data

In order to prepare a schedule, certain information must be available to the schedulers. First and foremost is the contract statement of work, commonly referred to as the SOW. The SOW describes the "what" to be produced. Quite often the SOW is a specification of the final thing the customer expects to get when the contract has been completed.

Next, the schedulers must obtain (or lay out for themselves) a listing of those tasks or activities which will be done in order to satisfy the SOW. The durations for each task must be assumed and the interrelationships of one task to another or several others must be estimated. This is the "how" of what will be done to satisfy the contract.

The "where" and "with what" of the job is represented by outlining which facilities and assets will be used to satisfy the SOW. If facilities are scarce and need to be leased, or purchased, or perhaps modified in some way, these tasks are a part of the "how" mentioned above. The cost of new capital equipment and other resources is also something to be considered and listed on the schedules under an event entitled: "management approval of capital assets."

The "who" to be responsible for the individual tasks is one of the more critical matters to be addressed in the preparation of a schedule. Until specific individuals are charged with performance responsibility for each known activity, jobs don't get done, or done on time. Schedules which not only display the work to be done and the time allowed, but also name the person who is to do the job, "the hangee," are more likely to get the appropriate people involved.

After the "what" and the "how" and the "where" and the "who" and the "with what" have been spelled out, the last issue to be settled is the "when," or what is commonly called the schedule. But where does schedule information normally come from?

If the schedulers are in luck most of their job will have been done for them and data will be available in a document typically called a "program plan," which might have been submitted earlier in a proposal to the customer. However, if no such plan exists the schedulers are left to their own resourcefulness to obtain the required information from whatever sources might be available to them.

Past jobs, the experiences of a company with similar work, are one of the best sources of reliable information to schedulers. If previous work has been recorded so as to allow a meaningful comparison with the new job, then management can be confident that the time spans shown on schedules will be realized. Any differences between an earlier job and the current job to be performed can be adjusted with the addition of an estimated complexity factor, the assumption that the current job is perhaps 10% more extensive, so therefore, a factor of ten percent more time will be allotted to its duration.

However, what if the company is new and has no past experience to draw from, or perhaps the new job is so different from all past work (pushing the state of the art) that no meaningful historical comparisons can be made. What then are the options available to the schedulers? A second possible approach to obtain the needed data is to get it from those persons given responsibility for the job. Those functional specialists who will be held responsible for a given task are likely to have the best understanding of what is involved in performing their tasks. The one danger of this source of data is that people will be people, and there is the possibility that some personal bias or "pad" will be included in the description of their respective efforts. Relying on data from personal interviews must be done with great care, and sometimes adjustments made for a given individual's optimism or conservatism.

Master Schedules

"The heart of the scheduling system is the master schedule."[1]

Before we get into the discussion of the various types of schedules in use, it might be beneficial to briefly touch on the subject of master schedules, what they represent, and how they should not be confused with schedule types. The term master schedule relates to its hierarchy, the placement of the schedule in a given program. It is synonymous with the term top schedule. Any type or form of schedule may be used to represent the top or master schedule. Gantt charts, milestone charts, and networks have all been used to display a master schedule for a program.

The key is that all master schedules must set the broad duration parameters for a program, and that all major subjects and

[1]"Design of the Scheduling System" by William E. Sandman, appearing in Chase and Aquilano, *Production and Operations Management* (Richard D. Irwin, Inc., Homewood, Illinois, 1981), page 426.

major milestones be included. On some master schedules, the managers responsible for major work segments are listed as a constant reminder of who will be doing the various activities. If a WBS was used in the planning of the program it is useful to have those significant WBS elements referenced by number on the published document. Figure 3-4 displays a typical master schedule for a developmental effort. A master schedule must be tailored to the particular effort being described.

Nearly half a century ago a definition of a master schedule was provided and interestingly, that description is as valid today as it was then:

> A master schedule is compiled to show, first, the total time available for the entire job if it must be finished by a certain time and, second, how the various portions of the job are to be scheduled.[2]

Types of Schedules in Use Today

A novice to the subject of scheduling is sometimes overwhelmed by the various types of scheduling configurations displayed, and the terms used to describe these displays. It might be helpful to point out that while schedules do travel under various titles and exotic terms, in fact, there are but three types of schedules in use today. They display the following or some combination of the following:

1-Activities or tasks (things that take place over a period of time).

2-Events or milestones (things that happen at a point/moment in time).

3-Dependencies or constraints (things that prevent something else from happening before that first thing completes).

Thus all schedules show one of the above, or some combination of the three.

---

[2]Charles A. Koepke, *Plant Production Control*, (John Wiley & Sons, Inc., New York, 1941), page 454.

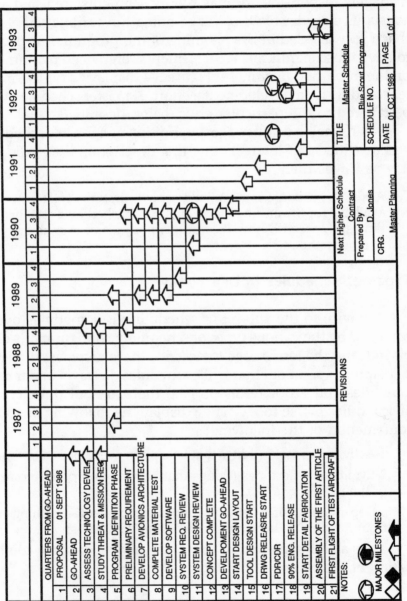

FIGURE 3-4 A TYPICAL MASTER SCHEDULE

The first category of schedules to be addressed are those which display activities. Earlier in this chapter we mentioned the Gantt chart, and a Gantt chart was shown in Figure 3-1. A Gantt Chart does nothing more than focus on activities or tasks and display them horizontally over a time scale. Quite often Gantt charts are called bar charts, which is perhaps a more descriptive term. Shown in Figure 3-5 is a bar chart. A bar chart, by any other name, is simply—a Gantt chart.

A second broad category of schedules reflect events or milestones (a milestone is a "big" event) and these are appropriately called milestone schedules or charts. A milestone chart is shown in Figure 3-6.

Notice the similarity between the activities displayed in Figure 3-5, the bar chart, and those events shown in Figure 3-6, the milestone chart. They are actually displaying the same job, the selected nine-month effort of Phase I of the hypothetical contract. Only the emphasis is different. The bar chart reflects the full duration of each of the tasks, whereas the milestone chart points only to the completion event at the end of each task. The method selected depends on the intended purpose of the schedule.

A project manager responsible for the Phase I portion of the contract might want to use a bar or Gantt chart to illustrate the effort and its status to upper management. The bar chart is also very useful in displaying information downward to a broad audience. By contrast, the customer may have elected to take this same information and incorporate it into the contract in the form of a milestone chart which only specifies the completion date of each of the tasks. The customer may not care when each task starts (that's the worry of the project manager) or how long they will take (that's also the responsibility of that person), as long as the total job completes as planned.

Now, having put all activities into tidy schedules called bar or Gantt charts, and all events into another schedule called a milestone chart, we are obligated to point out a simple truth: in practice there are very few "pure" bar or milestone charts

BAR CHART

ACTIVITY	JAN	FEB	MAR	APR	MAY	JUN	JUL	AUG	SEPT
CONTRACT SIGNING PROCESS	■								
PROGRAM PLANNING	■								
BILL OF MATERIAL DEVELOPMENT		▬							
SUBCONTRACTS SIGNING PROCESS			▭▬						
SYSTEM SPECIFICATIONS DEVELOPMENT				▭▬					
DESIGN REVIEW PROCESS					▭				
SUBSYSTEM TESTING						▭			
1st UNIT DELIVERY							▭		
PRODUCTION PLANNING								▭	
PROGRAM PHASE 1 COMPLETION									▭

FIGURE 3-5 A BAR CHART

MILESTONE CHART

EVENT	JAN	FEB	MAR	APR	MAY	JUN	JUL	AUG	SEPT
CONTRACT SIGNED	▲								
PROGRAM PLANNED	▲								
BILL OF MATERIAL FINALIZED			▲						
SUBCONTRACTS SIGNED			△▼						
SYSTEM SPECIFICATIONS FINALIZED				△ ▽					
DESIGN REVIEWED					△				
SUBSYSTEM TESTED						△			
1st UNIT DELIVERED							△		
PRODUCTION PLAN COMPLETED								△	
PROGRAM PHASE 1 COMPLETED									△

FIGURE 3-6 A MILESTONE CHART
Charts courtesy Humphreys & Associates, Inc.

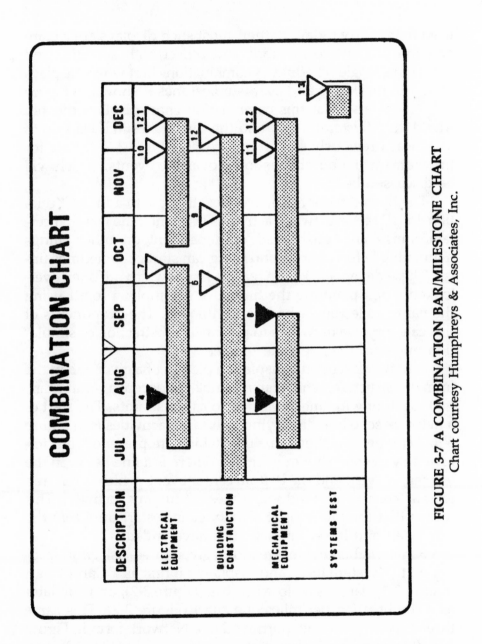

FIGURE 3-7 A COMBINATION BAR/MILESTONE CHART

Chart courtesy Humphreys & Associates, Inc.

used in industry today. Rather, most such displays are a combination of the two methods and reflect both activities and events in a single schedule. A combination chart which displays both activities/tasks and events/milestones is shown in Figure 3-7. Notice also that this combination chart displays our old friend the "Systems Test" and the three tasks that lead up to it, as was previously shown in Figures 3-1 and 3-2. Ignore for the moment the numbers shown over the events, which will be discussed below.

The third category of schedules attempts to add the "relationships" factor between activities or events, the fact that certain things are constrained or dependent on other things happening before that second thing can start or sometimes finish. These dependencies are real life issues which are often overlooked when planning the timing of a complex project using the bar or milestone schedule techniques. The proponents of this category use networks to portray an abstraction or simulation model of their real life project.

A network schedule displays a picture of a given job in the form of a structure, which can resemble in concept a Gantt chart, tied together with lines, referred to as constraints. The start of a network schedule displaying four tasks/activities is in Figure 3-8. Activities are shown as lines which are preceded and followed by events, shown in circles. There is a line between the top center event and the bottom center event, which is referred to as a "constraint" (and sometimes a "dummy" activity). This means that the lower right activity cannot start until *both* the upper left and lower left activities have ended.

Earlier in this chapter we took a given three-task effort leading up to "system test" and displayed it first as a Gantt Chart (Figure 3-1), later as a Flow Process (Figure 3-2), and still later as a combination bar/milestone chart (Figure 3-7). This same three-task effort is now portrayed in a Network form in Figure 3-9. "Systems Test," shown at the extreme right (12 to 13), cannot start until all three activities which lead into it have been completed, which is a real-life practical consideration.

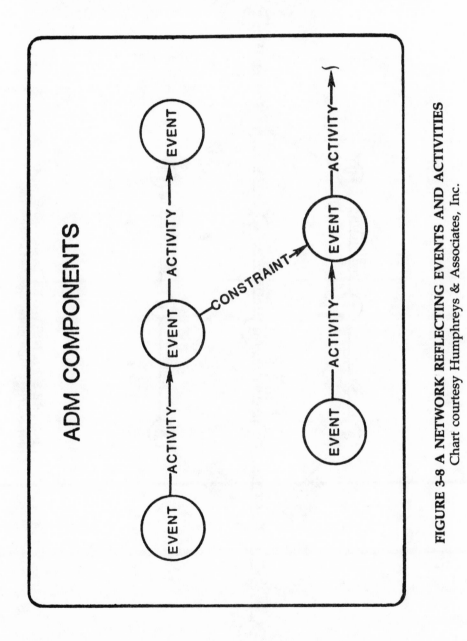

FIGURE 3-8 A NETWORK REFLECTING EVENTS AND ACTIVITIES
Chart courtesy Humphreys & Associates, Inc.

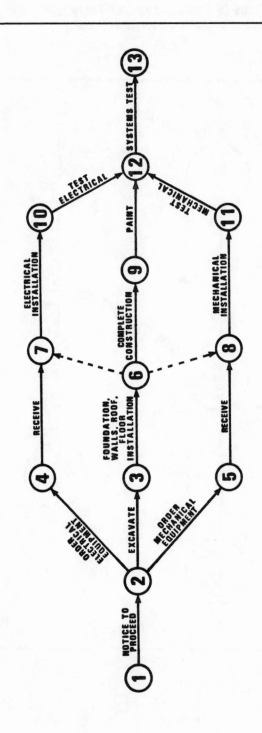

FIGURE 3-9 A NETWORK DIAGRAM
Chart courtesy Humphreys & Associates, Inc.

In this simple illustration such constraints may seem obvious. But in the heat of planning for a large and complex development, such critical issues are often overlooked. The value of network schedules is that they point out in clear terms the relationships which exist between seemingly unrelated tasks. Referring back to the Figure 3-9 illustration again, in order for the "Systems Test" to take place as planned, the electrical people, the mechanical people, and the facilities people must *all* work together as one team, and all complete their respective tasks as planned, or they will impact another person's task.

■ ■ ■

Our next chapter will deal specifically with some of the mechanics of Gantt and milestone charts. Then we will get into several chapters covering the important subject of network schedules.

Chapter 4

Gantt & Milestone Schedules

"Seeing changes take place in one plant after another, watching arbitrary management become democratic, and finding workman not only interested in their work but proud of it, strengthens the conviction that the Gantt chart is one of the most notable contributions to the art of management made in this generation."

Wallace Clark 1922[1]

The Gantt chart has been around for a long time. Many firms today still use the Gantt chart exclusively to schedule their work. There has to be some reason for its broad and continued acceptance for well over half a century.

Perhaps it's the simplicity of the Gantt chart which makes it so useful. Schedules are intended to enlighten, to convey information. When schedule information is presented using a Gantt chart, even if done poorly, the audience is likely to understand the message being sent.

Henry Lawrence Gantt was born in 1861. Prior to the end of the century he worked with Frederick W. Taylor, the father of scientific management, in his experiments at the Bethlehem

[1]Wallace Clark, *The Gantt Chart*, (The Ronald Company, New York, 1922); (Sir Isaac Pitman & Sons Ltd., London, 1934); translated and published in thirteen other countries.

Steel Company.[2] Later Gantt went his own way and during World War I conceived the institution we now refer to as the "Gantt chart."

The unique feature of the Gantt method is that can be used at all levels of the corporate structure. Top executives will use a Gantt display in presentations to their board of directors, where a mistaken point or badly conveyed message could cost them thousands of dollars in year-end bonuses. By contrast, Gantt charts are also used at the other end of the company to plan and measure the work of a machinist out in the factory.

Gantt charts work well in all industries, in all regions, in any culture, in any language. Even in those countries with languages which read from right to left (e.g. Arabic and Hebrew), they use Gantt charts presenting their schedule data left to right over a time scale. Gantt charts can be used to display a wide assortment of data: people, processes, machines, plants, developments, contracts, etc. And the time scales can portray minutes, hours, days, weeks, months, years, or even millennia for the historians.

But Gantt charts do not display dependencies, the relationship of one task to another. This is both a weakness in the technique and a benefit because it keeps the chart simple. When you have a Gantt chart which links tasks together with dependency lines you have in effect a network schedule, and we will be discussing the good and bad features of networks in the next few chapters. Many of the latest scheduling computer software packages have the ability to convert a network schedule display to a Gantt chart with the touch of a couple keys. The subject of automated scheduling will also be covered in a later chapter.

THE GANTT CHART

"The distinguishing feature of the Gantt chart is that work planned and work done are shown in the same space in their relation to each other and in their relation to time."[3]

There are numerous ways to display schedule data by use of a Gantt type chart, and typically, they are all correct. Few absolute rules apply, except for those specified in the above quote:

1 The discrete plan is displayed as a horizontal bar over a time scale.

2 Progress against the plan is shown in the same or a parallel bar, relating to the same time scale. With these simple rules people are able to convey their time plans in a clear and unambiguous manner.

The various symbols typically used in Gantt charts are shown in Figure 4-1. The original plan is shown as a split hollow bar. As progress is made against the plan, the top part of the hollow bar is filled in to the point where progress is made as of the "time now" date. The beauty of the Gantt chart is that progress as of the "time now" point can be clearly reflected. If results are on schedule, then the top section of the bar is shaded up to the "time now" point. Likewise, if the progress to date indicates that more or less time than was originally planned is now required, modifications to the original bar can be displayed as is reflected in Figure 4-1. Thus the Gantt chart can be used to display an original plan, present status against the plan, and also forecast any required changes to the plan. Simple but effective.

To better illustrate the various scenarios that are possible with a Gantt chart we will assume we have been awarded a one-year contract to design and deliver an article in a twelve-month period. We are halfway through the contract performance period and will use a Gantt chart to portray the original plan, and results against the plan. The Gantt chart used by our

[3]"The Gantt Chart", by Mrs. Wallace Clark, appearing in H.B.Maynard, *Industrial Engineering Handbook*, (New York:McGraw-Hill Book Company, Inc., 1956), pages 6-42.

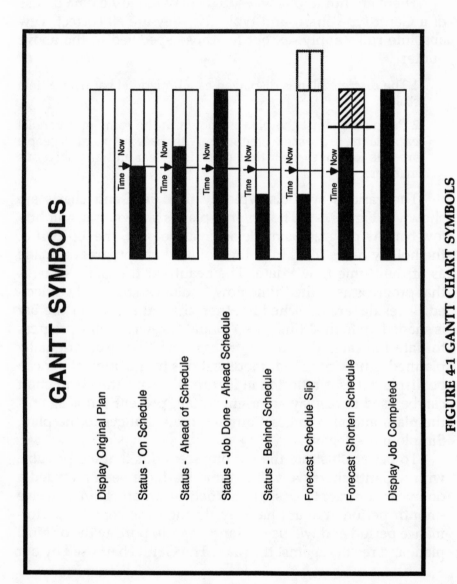

FIGURE 4-1 GANTT CHART SYMBOLS

program manager is shown in Figure 4-2. It is the same Gantt chart used six months earlier to display the planned approach to satisfy the new contract.

Figure 4-2 is reflecting progress through the month of June, the "time now" period. The discrete tasks are listed in the column on the left, and the time plan for each of these tasks is displayed under the time scale shown across the top. Notice that the tasks are listed in two broad groupings: those related to the design activities, and those related to building the article. Notice also that vendor quotes have slipped a week, but that all purchase orders were placed on time. All purchased materials should have been received as of the reporting "time now" period, but are now shown as slipping into the third week of July. However, the ship article date is still being shown as on schedule.

There is nothing absolute about the symbols or displays used in Figures 4-1 and 4-2. We have chosen a hollow split bar to reflect the plan, and progress reflected by shading in the top section. Some people prefer to show a single hollow bar and reflect progress by shading in the entire bar. Whatever works and conveys the intended message is correct with a Gantt chart.

THE MILESTONE CHART

The next schedule approach to be reviewed is called the milestone chart. This schedule, instead of portraying activities or tasks (Gantt charts), places its emphasis on events or moments in time. A milestone is by definition nothing more than a "big" or significant event which materially contributes to the completion of the project. But here the emphasis is placed on points of time, rather than focusing on the full duration of a task. Thus if the task of "design" is to be shown on a milestone chart, the events of "start design" and "complete design" would be displayed in place of the full task. Sometimes milestone charts reflect only the ending events, to keep the displays to a minimum.

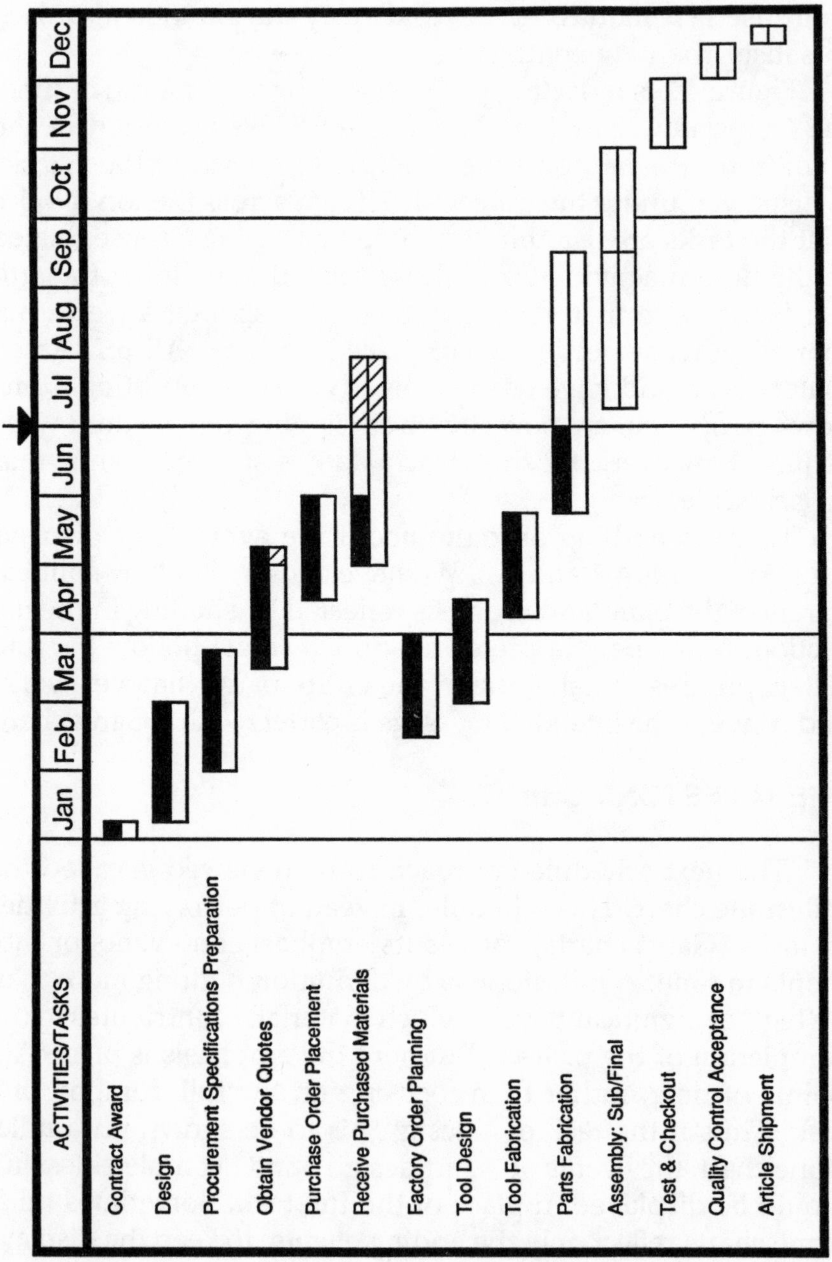

FIGURE 4-2 GANTT CHART

There is a difference between the symbols used in a Gantt chart and those used in a milestone chart. In Figure 4-3 we have taken the same eight examples we displayed earlier in Figure 4-1 to reflect Gantt characters, and have added the related milestone symbols. Note that some of the examples used in the Gantt charts are not available with the use of a milestone chart. While both schedule techniques can reflect a plan, the milestone chart cannot reflect status against the plan until the task listed has been completed, since most milestones focus only on the completion of the activity. The milestones listed can be expanded to show both the events of "start something" and "complete something" to better reflect some status, but the point is clear that a milestone chart is not as useful to reflect status conditions as is a Gantt chart.

The milestone chart is best used to focus on the "big picture," rather than dwell on progress along the way. Our same one-year contract to design and deliver a certain item is shown in Figure 4-4, only here we are displaying the same contract by focusing exclusively on the ending events. Notice that the sequence of work has been changed from the earlier Gantt display, because with a milestone chart all events are typically listed by date sequence. This approach leads to what is referred to as a "waterfall" display on the milestone chart, so named because the display curves downward from top left to lower right. However, milestone charts may also display data by WBS element, organization, function, or chronological sequence.

Top management sometimes prefers to watch a program using a milestone chart because there is no "subjectivity" allowed in the display: either a planned milestone has been completed on time, or it hasn't, in which case it will have to be rescheduled, typically with the use of a diamond symbol. Again, the symbols shown in Figure 4-3 are not absolutes, and some people prefer to show a planned event with an arrow pointing upward, which is quite acceptable.

If top management likes to see only the "big picture," customers also are likely to want to focus on an even higher top

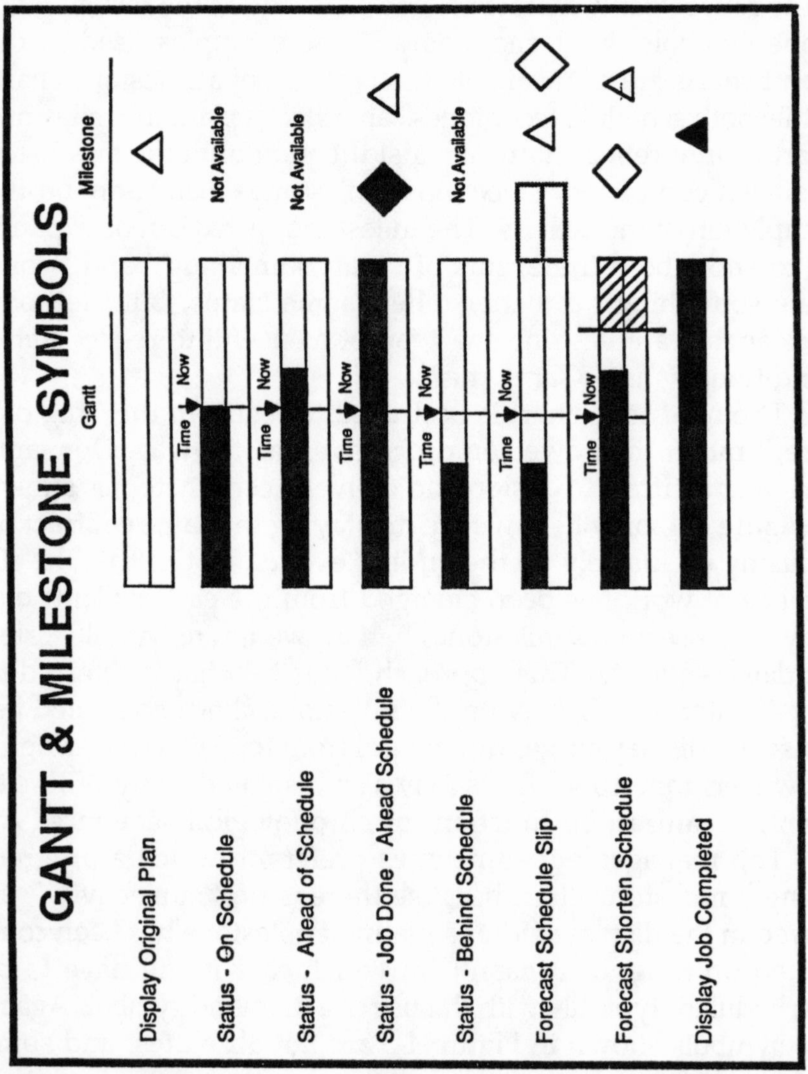

FIGURE 4-3 A COMPARISON OF GANTT & MILESTONE SYMBOLS

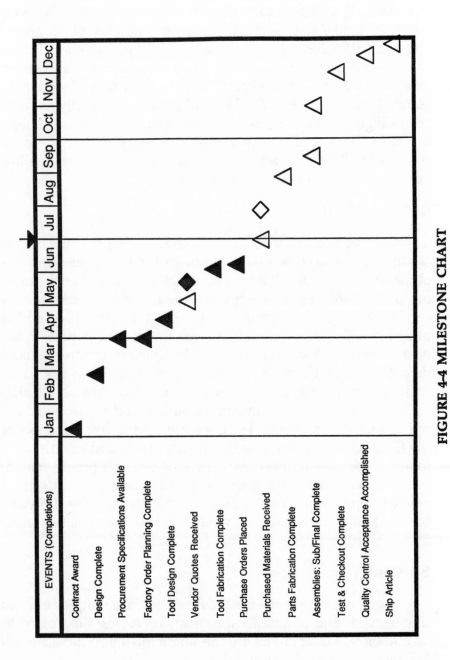

FIGURE 4-4 MILESTONE CHART

summary. It isn't that they are not interested, rather, a given customer is likely to be monitoring a multiplicity of programs and can't afford the time to review each in great detail. Therefore, customers may want only "major milestones" shown on progress reports sent to them, until events don't happen as planned, in which case additional information is usually requested. In Figure 4-5 our same one-year contract is shown reflecting only those events of a higher summary nature. Often a customer will incorporate "major milestones" as a separate appendix to the contract document itself.

Combination Charts

We have been describing two schedule approaches (Gantt & milestone charts) as if at some point the one ended and the other began. We did this only as a way of conveniently pointing out differences between the two. The differences in concept between an activity and an event will also have added meaning when we proceed to discuss network schedules in the next chapter. But in fact, in today's business world, we usually do not find pure Gantt or pure milestone schedules in use. Rather some combination of the two is more likely to be found.

In Figure 4-6 is our same one year contract is displayed using a combination chart. Here we are portraying the tasks of the Gantt chart reflected earlier in Figure 4-2, and also the customer major milestones shown in Figure 4-5. Our program manager has used the tasks from the Gantt display, because that was an appropriate display of the work planned for the year, but has added the milestones which the customer will be watching to monitor progress along the way.

SUMMARY

Gantt charts are useful because they are simple, easy to understand, and almost foolproof in conveying time plans to an audience. Gantt charts are the single most popular scheduling method in business today.

Milestone charts focus on the big picture. They are also good for presentations. Some customers incorporate major milestones in the contract document.

Neither the Gantt chart nor the milestone chart show dependencies, which is a shortcoming of both techniques. But both approaches are a useful initial step in the preparation of a network, which is the subject of our next chapter.

MILESTONES (Completions)	Jan	Feb	Mar	Apr	May	Jun	Jul	Aug	Sep	Oct	Nov	Dec
Contract Award												
Design Completed												
Procurement Specifications Available												
Purchased Materials Received												
Sub - Assembly Completed												
Final Assembly Completed												
First Article Shipped												

FIGURE 4-5 CUSTOMER MAJOR MILESTONE CHART

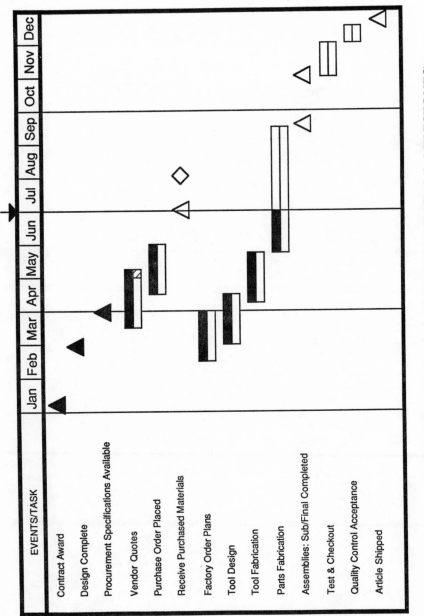

FIGURE 4-6 A COMBINATION CHART (SHOWING TASKS & MILESTONES)

Chapter 5

Network Schedules: Part 1
A Brief History

The next topic we will cover in some detail is network scheduling. It is an important subject. It is also a big subject. Therefore, we will break it up into several parts.

But before we get too far into the details of planning and managing a project using networks, it might be worthwhile to step back from the subject and briefly trace the history of the networking types which have been used since they were first introduced to industry nearly three decades ago. A multitude of similar but slightly different techniques initially emerged, and then later disappeared from use. At the time, their creators seemed to take great glee in announcing some exciting new system with an acronym title connoting "control." However, only three of the networking types had any lasting impact on business, one in name only. Today there are essentially only two network types in common use. It might be interesting to quickly review their evolution.

The three networking types we will discuss are: PERT, CPM/ADM, and PDM.

Program Evaluation and Review Technique (PERT)

PERT was first introduced by the United States Navy in 1958. It was a networking method developed for them by the management consulting firm of Booz, Allen and Hamilton for use on the Fleet Ballistic Missile Program, more commonly known as the Polaris Missile.

When introduced by the Navy, PERT was intended primarily for use as a "statistical" tool. PERT was to help determine whether or not the Polaris Missile would become operational within the needed time frame. Others took up the cause. They felt that PERT could be used as a "control" tool for use by management.

PERT received much publicity from its followers and was described as a technique which would revolutionize the entire business world. It fell far short of these expectations.

As a statistical tool PERT placed great emphasis on probability, the likelihood that something would happen as forecasted. The technique required three time estimates for each task in a network. These estimates were called: "the most likely," "optimistic," and "pessimistic." Those of us who had the misfortune of trying to coerce these three time estimates from overworked engineers and managers, deeply involved in their projects, quickly found that the method was unduly cumbersome. The effort required was greater than the resulting benefits. No matter what the "big boss," and possibly the customer, may have demanded, PERT as a management control technique was not viable.

Many government contracts in the early 1960s specifically required PERT and genuine attempts were made by many firms to comply with the requirement. Networks were dutifully submitted to satisfy the contractual need, but few used the networks in the management process. And before the technique of PERT (later called PERT-Time) became accepted by anyone but the management "theorists," its proponents added the cost dimension, and the tool became known as PERT-Cost. That announcement was the coup-de-grace for the technique.

But an interesting thing happened with PERT. While the technique never caught on with industry, the opposite happened with academicians. They immediately saw the potential in the concept and accepted the theory of network scheduling as a management tool. Many books were written on the subject of PERT. The subject was (and still is) taught in some university management courses. Interestingly, and in retrospect, both groups reacted to PERT in an appropriate way.

Industry properly rejected formal PERT, for as a practical tool it was too cumbersome to be of any value. Managements were too busy getting their jobs done to fool around with three time estimates.

Conversely, the academic community saw in PERT a valuable aid to management, if only some of the "bugs" could be worked out. They incorporated the concept into their curricula.

PERT as a technique is essentially gone from the American business scene. Yet today, when firms are asked if they use PERT, their reaction is generally affirmative. The reason is that the term "PERT" has become synonymous with networks. "It is not uncommon to have any network diagram designated a PERT chart, whether or not it truly is."[1] Thus the term PERT lives on to represent all networking approaches, although the actual method has long since disappeared. When people say they are using "PERT," they generally mean they are using networks with critical path methodology, employing one of the two accepted network types: arrow diagrams or precedence diagrams.

Critical Path Method (CPM), now know as Arrow Diagram Method (ADM)

CPM was initiated by the E.I. du Pont de Nemours Com pany about the same time as PERT, in 1957. Some authorities

[1]Milton D. Rosenau, Jr., *Successful Project Management*, (Belmont, California: Lifelong Learning Publications, 1981), page 63.

give credit for the technique to two gentlemen by the name of J. E. Kelly, Jr., and M. R. Walker.[2] No matter. Both techniques appear to be the product of, or to have benefited from, similar work done at M.I.T as early as 1946.[3] There were important differences in methodology between PERT and CPM when they were first introduced. These original differences quickly disappeared with the almost complete amalgamation of both techniques into a single one containing most of the features of CPM, but most often referred to as PERT!

While PERT was essentially rejected by the defense industry, commercial industry, particularly construction, immediately saw in CPM a valuable scheduling tool. One of the more important reasons for the acceptance of CPM was the fact that it is clearly activity oriented, and it is easily adapted to graphic displays. CPM is a simple concept to understand. By contrast PERT, with its heavy emphasis on statistical analysis and events, was not as easy to understand or visualize. Managers had to be specially oriented to be able to utilize the complex computer outputs, and most didn't bother.

It's funny the way names come into use. PERT was just plain PERT until PERT-Cost came along, then just plain PERT became PERT-Time. Much the same thing happened to CPM, which was later called ADM. Arrow diagrams didn't have a formal name until four or five years after they were in use. With the appearance of precedence diagrams, people started to use the terms ADM and PDM to differentiate between the two diagram types.

Arrow diagrams are the networking display method first used in the late 1950s to draw CPM networks. Geometrically,

[2]Elsayed A. Elsayed and Thomas O. Boucher, *Analysis and Control of Production Systems*, (Englewood Cliffs, New Jersey: Prentice-Hall, Inc., 1985), page 177.

[3]James J. O'Brien, *Scheduling Handbook*, (New York: McGraw-Hill Book Company, 1969), page 34.

they were represented by a line (arrow) with circles shown at each end of the arrow. The arrows represent activities, and the circles represent events.

Arrow diagrams place their emphasis on activities, and as such they can be displayed nicely over a time scale (by scaling the length of the arrow). Equally important, they are easy to understand even by people other than those who developed the network. The networks themselves are sometimes suitable for presentations, particularly when time scaled. In these instances they resemble a Gantt chart, but with connecting lines.

In the beginning, one of the cumbersome features of ADM was the event numbers. The very thing needed to communicate with the data processing machines made it difficult to communicate with the users. Without question, the single most important part of all networks is the logic. The logic has to represent the intended plan for the project. Often, in order to get a network to represent the plan it has to be calculated over and over several times. Each time the ADM network was changed the event numbers had to be changed. This was because the early ADM computer programs required that each successive event number be higher than the preceding number. ADM calculations were therefore slow and cumbersome. That type of condition is not good for fast moving, dynamic projects. Later improvements in ADM software have eliminated these difficulties.

Today ADM, earlier called CPM and sometimes IJ diagrams, is one of the two most widely used network types.

Precedence Diagram Method (PDM)

About five years after PERT and CPM/ADM came on the scene, the people at Stanford University came up with what they felt was a better approach to network logic and displays.[4]

---

[4] "Tools of Project Management," by Winfred Charette and Walter S. Halverson, appearing in Linn C. Struckenbruck, *The Implementation of Project Management: The Professional's Approach*, (Reading, Massachusetts: Addison-Wesley Publishing Company, 1981), page 121.

They did it to overcome some of the shortcomings found in ADM. They called their new approach the precedence diagram method, PDM for short.

Rather than portray an activity as a line preceded and followed by events (as with ADM), PDM places the activity into a geometric figure, called a node, typically represented as a rectangular box. All that is needed is to tie the various activities together with lines. The lines represent the relationship between the activities. A project plan can often be simulated with fewer activities and lines by using PDM rather than ADM.

Visualize for a moment an ADM network. All that can be shown are "finish-to-start" relationships between the activities. As one activity finishes, the next activity can begin. By contrast, PDM networks are able to display different types of relationships. "PDM adds 'start-to-start' and 'finish-to-finish' relationships (and others). This offers certain efficiencies in modeling concurrent tasks."[5]

Perhaps a summary display would help place these three network forms into perspective (see Figure 5-1).

Choosing the Type Of Network

While the decision on the particular network type effects all aspects of the project planning process, most schedulers either have no preference, or fail to exercise a knowledgeable and intentional choice. The choice of network type is between the two varieties available: arrow diagrams (ADM) or precedence diagrams (PDM).

A proper decision as to network type should be based on the expected nature of the project being planned. But, when an organization has an existing software program capable of producing only a single type of network, the scheduler often has a difficult time justifying expenditures for a different package. Other times, the existing computer hardware (perhaps

[5]Ibid.

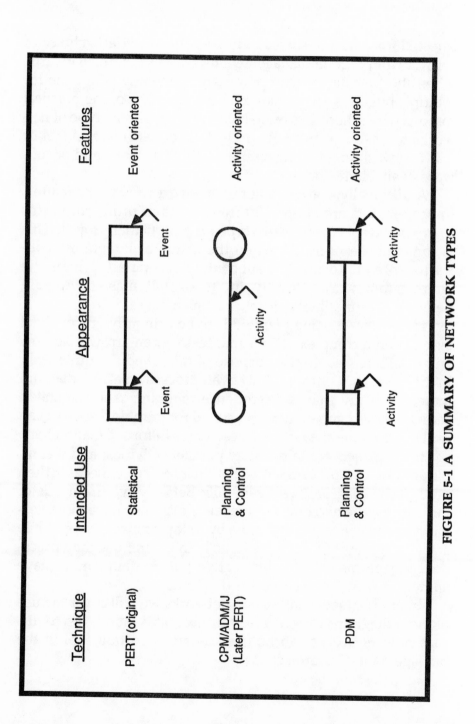

FIGURE 5-1 A SUMMARY OF NETWORK TYPES

selected for a non-business purpose) doesn't offer a choice of software for program management tasks. This is particularly true when the "available" computer isn't generally adaptable for multiple business applications. These are a few of the practical reasons why schedulers often have no choice in the type of networks to use to plan a new project. They use either ADM or PDM networks depending on the existing hardware and/or software available to them.

Additionally, the customer may have a voice in the matter. Subcontractors are often "directed" by their prime contractor to provide a specific network type for a particular project. This is sometimes a necessity when the prime or integrating contractor intends to use the subcontractor's data (perhaps the entire subnetwork) directly in its overall master program network. Compatibility dictates in such cases.

If the project being planned is to be primarily one of serial tasks, even a complex set of serial tasks, then arrow diagrams will most likely serve the purpose of the scheduler quite well. In this case, the computer may even process an arrow diagram more efficiently than a precedence diagram. And, as stated earlier, ADM is generally better suited for graphic displays than is PDM, because the network resembles in form a Gantt chart.

If the project contains many parallel activities, and if complicated or complex activity relationships are expected, then precedence diagrams will generally better serve the needs of the user. Of the two types, precedence diagrams have more flexibility and are most often chosen by today's newer users. While arrow diagrams (ADM) were initially in greater use than precedence diagrams (PDM), the relative position appears to have shifted in favor of precedence diagrams.

In our next few chapters on networks we will cover the use of these diagrams to plan a new project, and then go on to discuss how networks can be used as an important tool in the management of a project.

Chapter 6

Network Schedules: Part 2
Logic Diagram Basics

"A network is an abstraction of a real project"[1]

The use of logic diagrams to formulate a plan is a systematic and disciplined approach to preparing schedules. A logic diagram is a graphic portrayal of assumed work tasks and the relationships that are expected to exist between them, the sum of which makes up a whole thing, whether that whole thing be a project, a system, a job, an order, or whatever. The diagrams can be used to hypothesize relationships, to explore alternative approaches between various activities and events which make up a project, and to assist later in the management of an existing job. This method of planning and scheduling provides maximum assurances that a project has been thought out in a logical way, and that the resulting formal schedules represent a well defined and achievable way through to completion.

Network schedules, an offspring of logic diagrams, are particularly useful in the planning of projects which are new, or unique, or haven't been done before. They lend themselves

[1]James L. Riggs, *Production Systems: Planning, Analysis and Control*, (New York: John Wiley & Sons, Inc., 1981), page 221.

nicely to complex one-time-only efforts, and never-have-been-done-before jobs. Industrial managements which typically use logic networks prior to starting new work are those involved in construction projects, technical research contracts, and pharmaceutical developmental efforts, among others.

One of the more beneficial aspects of the use of logic diagrams in the planning for a new job is the forced communication which must take place between team members. Exploring and discussing the relationships of the components of a project provides team members with a better and more focused understanding of a project as a whole, and the part each will be expected to play in the overall undertaking. They must talk to each other and start to work together as a team, or the plan in the form of a logic diagram will never materialize.

As will be pointed out later, the use of logic diagrams to develop project schedules can be a tedious effort requiring much discipline, considerable mathematical calculation, and the continuing preparation of resulting graphic displays. All these processes lend themselves well to the use of automated data processing methods. In the past the mere volume of calculations presented a severe limitation on the use of network scheduling. The calculations, even when made by computer, were slow, required computer specialists (and other scarce resources), and typically produced voluminous (often user unfriendly) outputs. With the recent advances made in mini and microcomputers, and the numerous software packages specifically targeted at network scheduling, these difficulties have been greatly reduced. The use of logic diagrams to plan a project is now possible for anyone caring to undertake the effort.

A logic diagram is a plan which takes the physical form of a network expressing the anticipated tasks and their relationships to each other. In order to express such relationships, certain network attributes must be used. These attributes are discussed below in this order: "activities," "events," and the resulting "constraints" between them.

Activities

Logic diagrams which describe projects are primarily made up of activities. An activity is something (a task) that happens over time. Activities consume both time and other resources. Resources may take many forms, for example labor, material, supplies, and capital equipment, among other things.

Activities are commonly expressed through the use of active verbs. Examples of activities might include:

"prepare the drawing"

"cut the part to length"

"test the assembly using the test procedure"

"install the large valves on level 16"

"cure the concrete sub-flooring"

Notice that all of these activities represent specific tasks that are likely to be parts of larger tasks, which are in turn parts of larger tasks, and so forth. Also notice that all of these activities except for the last one consume other resources in addition to time. Concrete curing is an example of a somewhat unique activity, in that after the concrete is poured, the activity of "curing" happens without the requirement for other resources except for "time."

A Gantt chart describes a project by including all of the activities (or tasks) of the project. A logic diagram does the same thing. The principal differences are that the Gantt chart shows when the tasks will happen (the logic diagram does not), and the logic diagram shows how the activities are related to each other (the Gantt chart does not). This showing of relationships makes the logic diagram a "simulated model" of the project.

Events

An event is something that happens at a moment or point in time. In networking an event also represents a "state of being." It is contrasted with an activity, which happens over a period of time. Activities normally begin with an implied event of "start," and end with another event of "complete."

The activity mentioned earlier of "preparing the drawing" could also be expressed in an event oriented network with the use of the two events "drawing started" and "drawing completed." In most logic networks, events are not specifically called out since they are obvious from the description of the activity.

Important events which are critical to the overall project are elevated to the status of "milestone" or "key event" and are uniquely identified. Milestones are points in the project which identify significant and identifiable progress. They are both important and recognizable as major steps toward the overall goal of the project. These events are often the framework around which the entire project is undertaken. In the construction of a house, the events of "completion of design," "ground-breaking," "roof completion," "complete enclosure," and "complete final detail work" are examples of milestones in the path toward finishing the total effort. It is important to identify "milestones" to give them added emphasis.

In using a network to define a project, the majority of the events displayed are of a lesser significance and represent only the start or finish of individual activities. Such events are most often not specifically defined except by the logical assumption that one would apply to them as the start or finish of a certain activity. However, since the event that represents the completion of one activity will also represent the start of one or more other activities, it is necessary to consider the meaning of these events during the conceptualization of the network. Does the event of "drawing complete" also represent the start of the activity "place orders for material"? The answer to this question determines the correctness of the logic diagram. Descriptive titles of the events in a network need to be clear and unambiguous in order to ensure that all logical relationships are properly understood.

Most projects have one beginning and one end. While this is not always the case, it is desirable that all logic diagrams or networks have a single defined beginning and a single defined end. Some computer programs also require a single beginning and single end. Beyond these simple restrictions, the team defining their project in the form of a logic diagram is free to place the emphasis where they choose.

Constraints

Constraints represent logical relationships between two or more events or activities. They are used to establish the condition whereby one event (or activity) must precede another. Thus a constraint is a "limitation or restriction on actions."[2] Constraints are a vital element in a representative plan. They are often overlooked when the more traditional scheduling methods (e.g. Gantt charts) are used.

There are several types of constraints used in logic diagrams. The first one we will review is called an "absolute constraint."

Absolute Constraint

An absolute constraint displays a logical relationship. There are many situations (in both ADM and PDM) where the constraint must be displayed to accurately represent the true project plan. Figure 6-1 illustrates four tasks and the constraint which exists between activities AC and BD.

Figure 6-2 takes this same logical relationship and adds actual task descriptions. The project goal is to raise the flag (Activity C). But to complete the total job the landscaping must be replaced (Activity D). The landscaping cannot be replaced until the pole hass been erected and the landscape materials have been purchased.

[2]Jack R. Meredith and Thomas E. Gibbs, *The Management of Operations*, (New York: John Wiley & Sons, 1984), page 669.

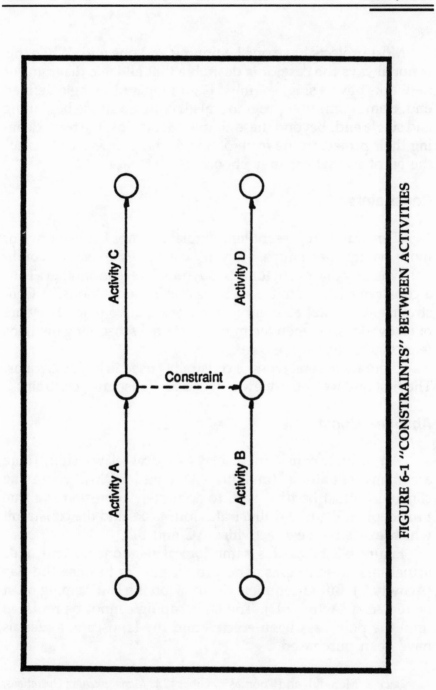

FIGURE 6-1 "CONSTRAINTS" BETWEEN ACTIVITIES

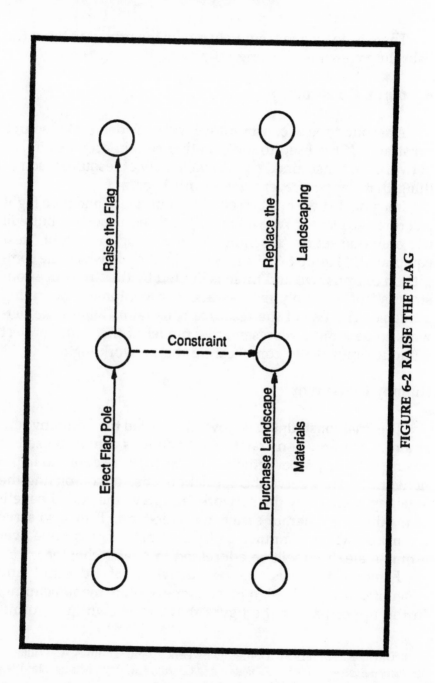

FIGURE 6-2 RAISE THE FLAG

There is no way to accurately model the project without the "absolute constraint" being reflected.

Resource Constraint

A second type of constraint we will consider is a "resource constraint." It is used to indicate that certain activities in the network are constrained by the availability of resources, something that happens every day of our lives.

Imagine that we must assemble, ground test, and then flight test three airplanes. We will build the three airplanes, but will use only one set of "assembly fixtures" and one set of "test equipment." Figure 6-3 displays the situation in which the completion of units two and three is limited by the "resource constraints" of assembly fixtures and test equipment becoming available. The use of the resource constraints allows the network to be a more representative model of the actual project without significantly complicating the network logic.

Dummy Constraint

The final constraint to be covered is called the "dummy constraint." Dummy constraints are "fictitious activities used to ensure that the proper activity relationships are depicted in the network."[3] They serve the special purpose of completing the logic represented by the network, and have the added benefit of making the diagram easier to understand. They also serve a purpose when computer plotting of networks is done over a time scale. This will be addressed in a later chapter.

Figure 6-4 shows the two activities of "design" and "manufacturing." Design must happen before manufacturing. In the upper part of the figure they are shown in a normal

---

[3]David R. Anderson, Dennis J. Sweeney, and Thomas A. Williams, *Production Systems: Planning, Analysis and Control*, (St. Paul, Minnesota: West Publishing Company, 1982), page 345.

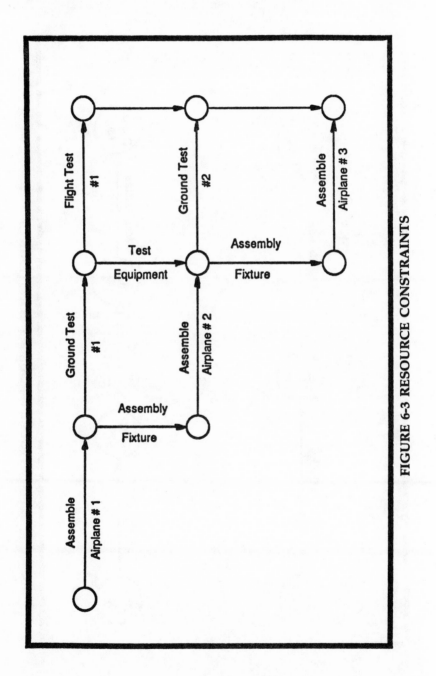

FIGURE 6-3 RESOURCE CONSTRAINTS

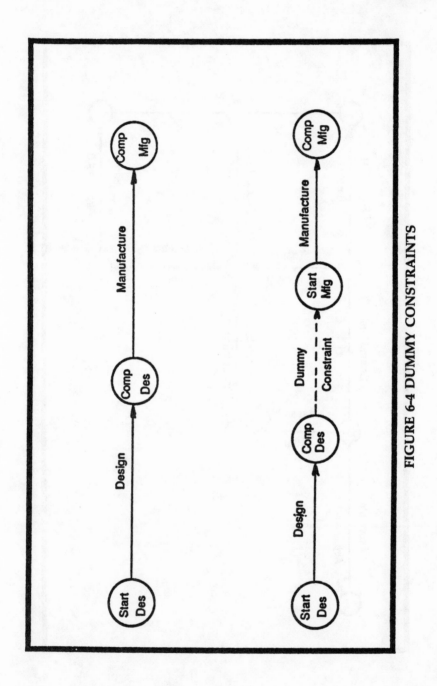

FIGURE 6-4 DUMMY CONSTRAINTS

manner. But in the lower part of the figure, the event "start manufacturing" has been added, together with the "dummy constraint." This helps present a truer model of the logic to explain, for example, that design might complete at one point in time, but that manufacturing might not immediately start.

Logic Diagram Relationships

The relationships between the various activities, events, and constraints displayed in a diagram are the things that simulate the plan for a project. A list of all the activities which are contained in a network would provide a "statement of work" of sorts for the project. The logic of the diagram shows how the various pieces fit together to form the whole. There are a number of ways to display the various relationships which can occur. We will show some of these possibilities.

Parallel Activities

Two or more activities may start from a single point and end at the same point, but during their term they happen independent of each other. These are called "parallel" activities and are illustrated in Figure 6-5. They are not so independent that they can be done at any time. Rather, they both start from a single event and their completion signals a single event. They must happen at approximately the same time. Beyond that, they are independent of each other. An example of parallel activities is the work of the various musicians in an orchestra. They all begin together and end together (hopefully), but in the meantime they perform their different tasks.

Sequential Activities

Other activities may occur in a series, or in a sequential way. Figure 6-6 illustrates a sequential flow of activities. This relationship is used to describe tasks that logically happen one after

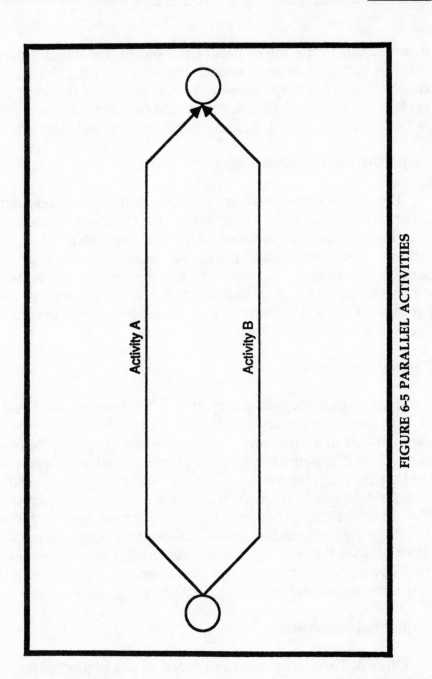

FIGURE 6-5 PARALLEL ACTIVITIES

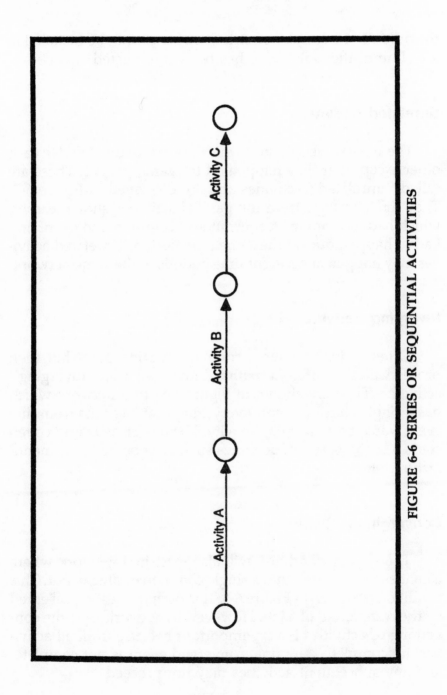

FIGURE 6-6 SERIES OR SEQUENTIAL ACTIVITIES

the other. For example, electrical wiring cannot be installed in a wall until the wall frame has been constructed.

Unrelated Activities

There are some activities which are totally unrelated to each other except that they happen on the same project. These are called "unrelated" activities and are displayed in Figure 6-7. They differ in logic from the parallel activities shown earlier, which had a common start event and common end event and had to happen during the same time period. Unrelated activities may happen at different time periods in the same network.

Diverging Activities

Often activities have a common starting point but then proceed along different paths. These we call "diverging" activities. They are shown in Figure 6-8. In a network which has a single starting point, everything that happens from that event would be a diverging activity. The release of a design often starts a broad series of activities such as procurement, manufacture, etc.

Converging Activities

The reverse condition will also exist in a network where activities "converge" into a single common ending event. This condition is shown in Figure 6-9. It is perhaps best represented by the completion of a job. However, in network logic the converging of activities is very important because until all activities are completed the final converged event is not complete, and any subsequent activities may not proceed.

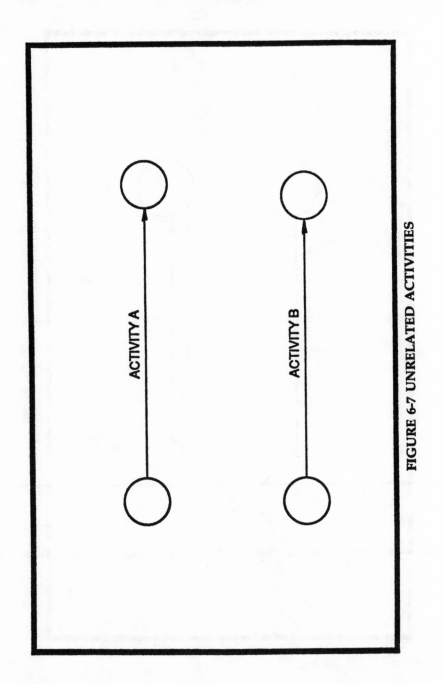

ACTIVITY A

ACTIVITY B

FIGURE 6-7 UNRELATED ACTIVITIES

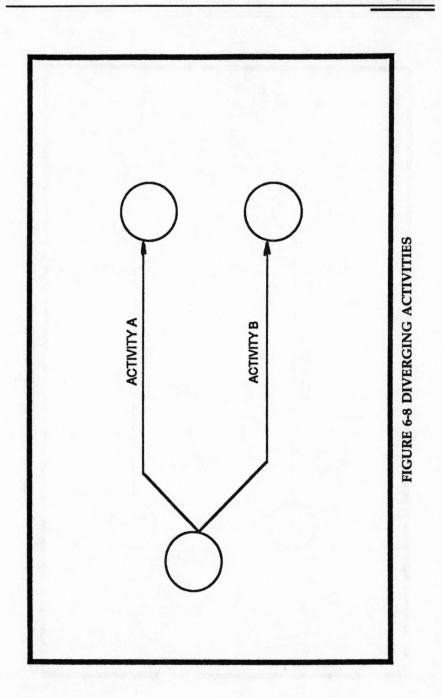

FIGURE 6-8 DIVERGING ACTIVITIES

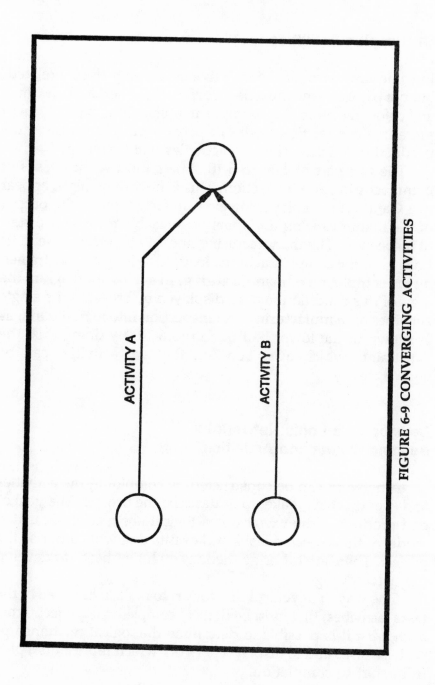

FIGURE 6-9 CONVERGING ACTIVITIES

Overlapping Activities

In some cases two (or more) activities are very closely related, but not parallel. One must begin before the other, and one must end before the other. For example, manufacturing typically takes place in close relation to the inspection process on the same production articles. The two activities will "overlap."

The top part of Figure 6-10 shows the two processes of manufacturing and inspection. This is how they might appear in a Gantt-type display. However, in fact, some of the output of the manufacturing line must be available prior to the start of inspection. The manufacturing line will then continue to its finish, but the completion of the inspection is again constrained by the completion of manufacturing. In a network diagram the logic of this condition may be displayed by breaking the single activities of manufacturing and inspection into logical parts, as is shown in the lower half of Figure 6-10. By doing this, the constraints which exist between the two activities can be shown clearly.

Developing a Logic Network by
Relating Events and Activities

A network can be constructed by combining the activities and events which make up or describe the project. The goal or end product of the exercise is a logical abstract or simulated model of the expected tasks and events that will comprise the project. There are differing theories on how "best" to develop the network logic.

One way to develop a network is to make a list of all of the tasks (activities) that must be done to complete the project. From such a list it is possible to determine the logical relationships of these tasks and to display a network which represents a plan from start to completion.

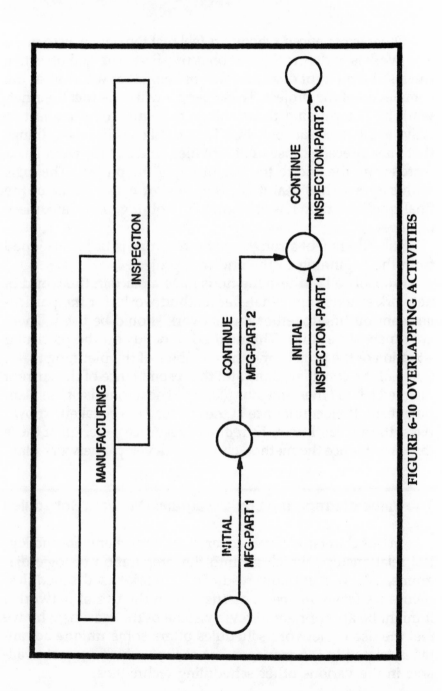

FIGURE 6-10 OVERLAPPING ACTIVITIES

Other experienced schedulers feel that the only way to make a network is to define the end objective first. The end objective can also be thought of as the state of being that will exist at the completion of the project. These people will construct their network by determining those things that must be done last to arrive at the final state of being. They must consider those things that must precede those final activities, and so they work backwards from the end to the beginning of the project. The logic of this approach is that it is easier to start with an idea of the final condition than it is to begin with nothing, or a blank piece of paper.

Still others feel strongly that a network is best developed from the beginning to the end of a project.

Probably all of these methods have a place in the world of network scheduling. Whatever method works for the particular team putting together the network should be used. There are no absolute rules. The method depends on the particular situation of the project and the members of the planning team. Some of the considerations are: the resemblance of the current planned job to other previous jobs, the backgrounds of the planning team, their confidence in the approach to be taken, known risks, the availability of the required resources, etc. All of these things influence the method chosen to develop a network plan.

The Value of Preparing Logic Diagrams/Network Schedules

In this chapter we have covered the basic elements and logical relationships which go into the preparation of logic diagrams, which eventually result in network-based schedules. Before we leave this basic discussion on the use of networks, it might be appropriate to review some of the reasons why we feel the use of network schedules offers some unique advantages related to the management of time which are not available in the various other scheduling techniques.

The use of logic diagrams to plan and manage a project provides the following benefits:

1) It encourages (forces) planning and communication between team members;
2) It lays out the tasks, points out interrelationships, shows the individual responsibilities of team members;
3) It helps to highlight and focus on problem areas;
4) It helps management examine resources: scarce resources, surplus resources, inefficient utilization and/or resources out of phase with the requirements of the project;
5) It supports alternative solutions for management's consideration.

Chapter 7

Network Schedules: Part 3
Planning A Project

We are now ready to continue with the basic ideas covered in the last chapter on logic diagrams. We will discuss the planning of a project using a logic network. The network can be an invaluable tool when used to define the essential relationships that are expected to exist in a project, and to organize the planned tasks and their expected time durations.

Out of this network development will come a tentative project plan in the form of a logic diagram. The "critical path" will be derived from this plan. The exact location and content of the critical path must be known and verified on every project, for it will serve as the basis for management decisions with respect to the allocation of and timing of project resources. Once the phasing of the project has been accomplished and the required resources evaluated, a "schedule baseline" can be established. The schedule baseline will serve as a reference point during the life of a project and for use in controlling it.

The actual development of a schedule and the management of the project with the aid of a network will be the subjects of the final chapters on network scheduling.

CONSTRUCTING THE NETWORK

Using the Arrow Diagram Method (ADM)

Arrow Diagrams consist of arrows (lines with arrowheads to designate the direction of flow) to represent the activities of the project, and geometric symbols (typically circles referred to as "nodes") to represent events that occur both before and after each activity. Using this networking form, any and all of the relationships that were previously described can be represented. See Figure 7-1 for an example of an arrow diagram.

Activity descriptions are placed on the arrows. Events are usually not described. In these networks the activities are identified by the pair of event nodes that bound them. The common practice is to name the untitled events by using an event number and to identify the activities by using their preceding and succeeding event nodes. For example, in Figure 7-2 the activity "Replace the Landscaping" would be identified as "Activity 538-556." If the figure looks familiar it should. It was used in the last chapter on logic diagrams, but without the identifying ADM characteristics.

ADM can also be applied using a network in which the *events* are described. This was the approach used by many of the early PERT practitioners. While these are still activity networks, they are highly event oriented. The events are described, and for the most part the nature of the activity between events is assumed. However, the activity is still the focus of the critical path analysis since it is the basis of the consumption of time. This method has since fallen from favor and is not used for practical purposes today.

In the early years of arrow diagrams (and in some quarters today) ADM networks were referred to as "IJ diagrams." In this usage the "I" stood for the "input" event to the left (or beginning) of an activity, and "J" considered the "juncture" event to the right (or end) of the activity. Each of the events was given a number. For example, the activity "design the

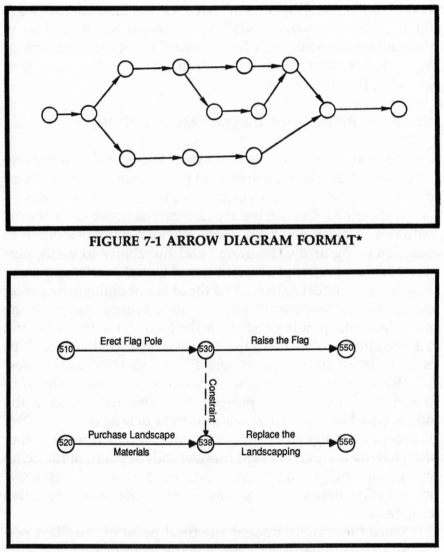

FIGURE 7-1 ARROW DIAGRAM FORMAT*

FIGURE 7-2 "ACTIVITY 538-556"

*All charts in this chapter courtesy of Humphreys & Associates, Inc.

patio," would be shown on the network as a line, preceded and followed by numbered nodes. These might be referred to by the schedulers as the "158/479" activity. Great for communicating with a computer, but not so useful when discussing a project with the builder.

Using the Precedence Diagram Method (PDM)

As was mentioned earlier, the Precedence Diagraming Method was developed subsequent to the arrow method. It was developed primarily to overcome some of the limitations of arrow diagrams. Certain types of logical relationships that exist between project activities were difficult (cumbersome) to describe using arrow diagrams, and the ability to easily portray additional types of constraints and logical relationships was sought. In an effort to overcome these shortcomings the precedence method was conceived. The underlying principle of the precedence diagraming method is the focus on the activity, and the meaning of the constraint, or relationship identifier. This is the primary difference between PDM and ADM approaches.

PDM uses activities and constraints (or relationships) to describe the logic of the project. Activities are placed in the nodes which contain their work content description. In PDM, numbers are assigned to the node containing the activity, rather than having a separate event number independent of the activity, as with ADM. The graphic form used to describe an activity in a PDM network is typically a rectangular box, also called a node.

Since the activity node is the focal point of the PDM network, all that remains is to describe the relationships that exist between the activities. These relationships are called constraints. They are represented by lines drawn between activity nodes. As will be mentioned throughout this chapter, PDM networks allow much more specific definition to be used to describe various relationships between activities.

Figure 7-3 is an example of a PDM network. This network illustrates five distinct activity relationships which are possible using PDM: finish-to-start; start-to-start; finish-to-finish; start-to-finish; and partial start or finish.

Activity Relationships

A "finish-to-start" relationship constraint implies that the preceding activity must be completely finished before the succeeding activity can even begin. See Figure 7-4 for such a relationship using PDM. This relationship is used in the sequential or serial flow of activities in arrow diagrams. It is the only relationship which can be used with ADM. Observe in Figure 7-3 that "finish-to-start" relationships exist between activities D-G, C-E, and F-H.

An example of a finish-to-start relationship might be that of washing a batch of clothes, and then going on to dry the same batch. The washing must be completely finished before drying can be started. There is no possibility of the two activities being done at the same time, though there might be some delay between the two activities.

A "start-to-start" relationship can also be used with the logic of a PDM network. This implies that the start of one activity constrains the start of the second activity. See Figure 7-5 for such a display using PDM.

An example of a start-to-start relationship can be visualized in a foundation construction job. The relationship between the placement of rebar and the pouring of the concrete for a large foundation can be one of start-to-start. After the first area of the rebar has been placed, the cement pour activity can begin. It is not necessary to wait for the entire rebar placement to be completed to begin the pouring of cement. Four start-to-start relationships are shown in Figure 7-3 between activities A-B, B-D, E-F, and G-F.

A "finish-to-finish" relationship can also be represented with PDM. This relationship suggests that one activity must

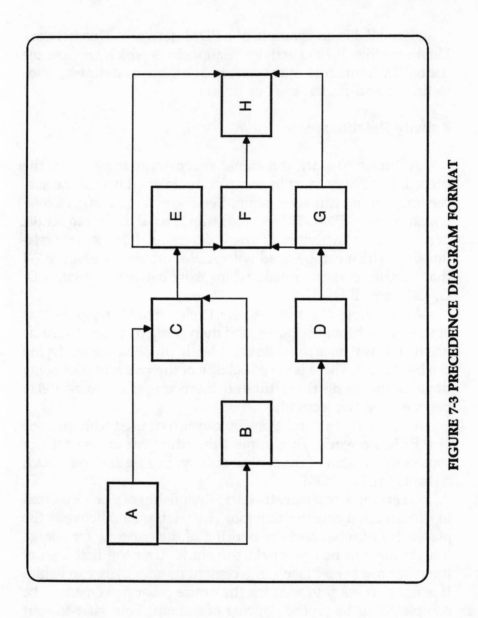

FIGURE 7-3 PRECEDENCE DIAGRAM FORMAT

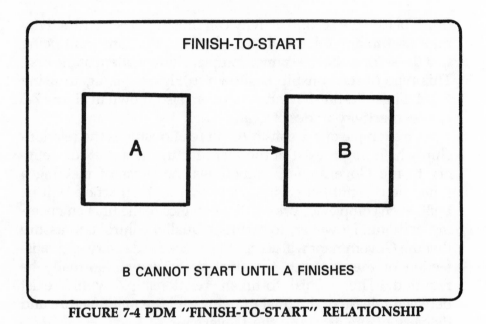

FIGURE 7-4 PDM "FINISH-TO-START" RELATIONSHIP

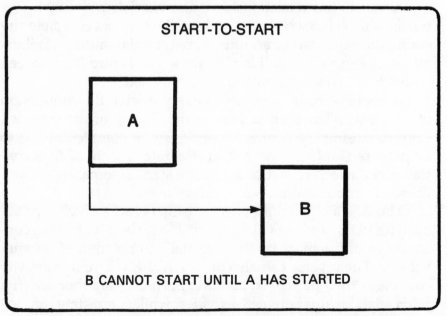

FIGURE 7-5 PDM "START-TO-START" RELATIONSHIP

finish before the second activity can finish. The second activity may start in any relationship to the first, the constraint being that the second activity cannot complete independent of the first. This type of relationship is shown in Figure 7-6, again using PDM. Finish-to-finish relationships are also shown in Figure 7-3 between activity nodes B-C and G-H.

An example of a finish-to-finish relationship is the relationship which might exist in the manufacture of a unit for delivery to the Government. Sometimes the press of meeting a schedule commitment will dictate that a given article will be built, even completed, prior to the issuance of the final engineering drawing. However, to maintain quality control and assure that the Government will accept the article for delivery and satisfaction of the contract, the final drawing will normally be required. Thus, finish-to-finish relationships would exist between release of the final drawing and the manufacture and delivery of the article to the Government.

A start-to-finish relationship is also possible with PDM. This relationship exists when a second activity may not complete any earlier than the start of another activity. This condition is illustrated in Figure 7-7, and is also shown in Figure 7-3 between nodes E-H. This relationship is rarely used.

A start-to-finish relationship might exist at the completion of a contract. The final activity is the closing of the contract. Prior to closing the contract a certificate of completion has to be prepared and approved. Thus the relationship of final contract completion is constrained by the start of preparing the certificate of completion. Again, rarely used.

There is one remaining relationship (a fifth) which is possible with PDM, and we will only touch on it briefly. It is the constraint of one activity by the "partial" completion of another activity. The reverse can also be described, where one activity constrains the "partial" remaining portion of another activity. Such relationships between activities, while interesting, are seldom used and rarely allowed (we know of none) with computer software. We do not recommend the use of this type of

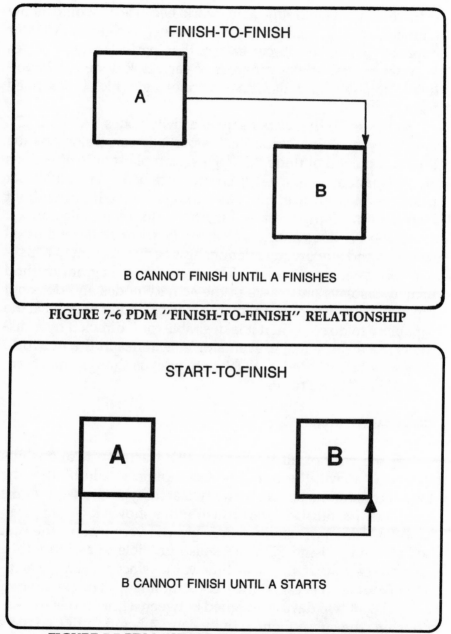

FINISH-TO-FINISH

A

B

B CANNOT FINISH UNTIL A FINISHES

FIGURE 7-6 PDM "FINISH-TO-FINISH" RELATIONSHIP

START-TO-FINISH

A

B

B CANNOT FINISH UNTIL A STARTS

FIGURE 7-7 PDM "START-TO-FINISH" RELATIONSHIP

constraint in developing a network because it would allow ambiguous relationships to exist between activities. A better approach would be to break each of the "partial" activity nodes into two nodes, where progress of each task node can be followed precisely, or to use the constraint lag, which is described below.

In Figure 7-3 the relationship of activity nodes "A" and "C" illustrates the point. Node "C" is partially constrained by the final completion of node "A." This example is only offered as an explanation of what a PDM network may display, and is not recommended for use. Life has enough uncertainties without incorporating intrigue or ambiguities into a logic diagram.

Using PDM, an entire project can be planned describing all activities and any unique relationships between them in a manner not possible with ADM. The precedence diagram method usually displays only tasks in the activity nodes and does not typically display events (moments in time). But it does have the capability to do so. When it is desirable (or if directed by a customer) to include major events or milestones in the network, they may be included in PDM networks as though they were "zero time" activity nodes.

Constraint Lags

In the case of all five of the PDM activity relationships described above, the ordinary assumption would be that the logical constraints between any two activity nodes would take zero time. If a finish-to-start constraint is shown it would mean that the following activity can begin the very instant the first activity ends. Using PDM, it is also possible to assign a time span to the constraints. This time value (since no activity actually takes place) is called the "constraint lag." For example, if a time lag of two days is assigned between a finish-to-start relationship, the subsequent activity cannot begin until two days after the first one has completed. Constraint lags are commonly used to display such things as curing time for concrete foundations or part movements from one factory location to another.

Approaches to Developing the Logic

There are a number of different methods used to develop network logic, and various seasoned schedulers have their own strong preferences. Some prefer to develop networks from inputs solicited from the assigned project participants, and/or to interview experienced individuals in organizations who have participated in similar efforts. Others like to gather their data from project documents (proposals, specifications, work statements, directives, etc.). Still other schedulers prefer to develop the detailed network logic through repeated (downward) expansions of subordinate summary networks. This expanding downward can be done for the entire project at one time, or on jobs of a long duration, timed to coincide with important future events, as when a "rolling wave" concept is used. As early milestones are reached, the next project phase is then planned in detail, as with a "rolling wave."

While using these various approaches some experienced schedulers insist that the only viable way to construct a new network is to start with the last activity of the project, and work backwards, asking the question, "What must come before this?" This is called backward scheduling.

This group insists that their preferred method is the best and surest way to develop an all-inclusive project network.

Other schedulers, equally as experienced, insist that the reverse process is the better way to undertake the planning task. They begin with the first project event and work their way forward asking, "What comes next?" These people feel just as strongly about the benefits of their forward scheduling approach.

Some project teams are very adept at forming subgroups to develop portions of the network for a particular task or a component of the total effort. This approach works best when the team participants have previously worked together. When all team members have a good understanding of the individual contributions to be made by the other members of the group, a project network is quickly synthesized.

A truly representative project network is ordinarily a team effort, and rarely developed by one or two individuals off somewhere by themselves. One of the principal reasons for this is that in addition to the final objective of producing a project network, the intent of the exercise is to place responsibility for task performance and to get the group into the habit of working together as a team.

At least one other approach is frequently used to develop logic diagrams. This is the development of independent subnetworks (clusters of related tasks) which describe a given task or project area. As these subnetworks are expanded, the evolving network and time frames can be related to the next higher level network. This approach can be used in concert with any of the other methods described above. It is particularly useful when management wants to focus on "risk areas" of a program, i.e., where there is uncertainty or a question as to whether or not a critically needed element will be available to the project as planned. For example, a new radar may be essential to the full scale development of an advanced fighter aircraft, and as such, would be a likely candidate for the independent development of a subnetwork.

In addition to choices regarding the logic development, the overall structure of the network(s) must be thought through. Will the project be planned and controlled using a single network, or will a group of individual but related networks be used? What summarizations of the detailed data will be made to create higher level management displays? Questions such as these should be answered in advance to determine the structure of the network(s) being considered.

Many times the size of an individual network, measured by the number of activities contained therein, is constrained by any one of a number of extrinsic issues, including the graphics plotter available, which constrains the ability to draw the network being produced. Other times constraints are caused by the need to subdivide the work into manageable organizational elements, sometimes separated by geographical locations of the project team members. If an integrated set of subnetworks (or fragnets) are to be used, then some overall plan must be devised for "hooking" networks together by making connector (constraint) lines which go from one subnetwork to another. Plans such as these can, and often are, derived after the project starts. But they serve the scheduler and the project better if they are considered before starting the effort.

Enough of logic and theory. It is time to develop a real life schedule, the subject of our next chapter.

Chapter 8

Network Schedules: Part 4
Developing The Schedule

Once the preliminary logic has been established, a number of additional steps must be taken to transform the network into a "project schedule." Time spans must be estimated for all of the tasks/activities contained in the network; the critical path must be isolated; and the requested resources must be analyzed. Only after each of these steps has been carried out can the network be considered as representative of a baseline schedule position. Each of these steps will be considered in detail.

Estimating Time Spans

Estimating time durations is one of the most important tasks involved in schedule development. This should be done by those persons who will ultimately be responsible for the project, i.e., those who must perform according to the commitments being made. As we shall see below, estimating proper time durations will have as great an influence on the establishment of the critical path, and on the eventual release of a realistic project schedule, as will the actual logic contained in the network itself. There are a number of methods typically used to estimate time durations.

In many cases, particularly with mature firms in a relatively stable business, many of the tasks being planned in the logic network have been done before on other company projects. In some industries (e.g. residential construction) and with some individual companies, data bases have been established and are maintained which contain duration spans from previous jobs. Data of this type can be invaluable for comparison with specific new tasks, or for parametrically estimating a range of tasks. In such cases, these statistics are the primary source of the time duration estimates. When such statistics are used, attention must be paid to the selection of data for comparison and the comparability of the task. The availability of such historical data sometimes causes the scheduler and other responsible individuals to place too much reliance on these data, without proper regard to their applicability. Past experience is useful for comparison, but only if it is intelligently applied.

In some instances, estimated labor hours can be used to develop time spans. In some manufacturing industries, labor consumption estimates (sometimes estimated with "engineered standards") and sequential flows (plans that identify tasks and movements from operation to operation) can be used to develop time durations. Often this is done using algorithms for the conversion. These algorithms may take into account various factors, including the actual task accomplishment, the movement between operations, and a pre-planned "bank" or queue to compensate for such typically experienced delays as waiting times, setup times for tools, machine availability, etc., to mention only a few.

When a data base of this type is not available, the individuals responsible for estimating time spans must use their past experiences and backgrounds to determine the most likely forecasted durations for the planned work. When this approach is used the accuracy of the project plan is often affected in one of two opposite ways.

First, people estimating a new job with limited actual experience will have a tendency to be optimistic. They have no way to fully grasp the true meaning of a never-been-done-before job. Their estimated time durations are likely to be too short because of their lack of a full appreciation of the effort being planned.

Second, the more senior people, who may still lack experience on a particular task, will have a tendency to be conservative. They are likely to add a safety "pad" to their estimates, perhaps remembering bitter experiences from past jobs. Therefore, these time durations will be off in the opposite direction. Selecting the process for arriving at a realistic and accurate time estimate for a new job is clearly a critical aspect of project schedule development.

One sound way to add confidence to a new job estimate is to have management go through a detailed, in-depth review of the proposal—before the commitment is made. Particular attention should be placed on those areas of the total effort where the company has little past experience with which to make a valid comparison.

Also, it is usually advisable to document (if only for the record) the expected conditions and basic assumptions that are used when the logic and time durations are developed. This rule applies regardless of the method used to develop the estimates. This approach will provide a framework for comparison and, hopefully, for making later improvements on other work. As the new project progresses, time durations for later tasks should be periodically reviewed. When this is done, the ground rules and assumptions that were originally used to develop the durations can be compared, and future durations changed where appropriate. The prudent documentation of original basic assumptions and time duration estimates can help to avoid one of the most common abuses of networking: the arbitrary shortening of future time durations (work to go) to compensate for current delays (work completed), with no sound basis for the change in duration spans.

When developing the time estimates for a new network, the selected unit of measure should be given some thought. Many of the existing computer programs require that an entire network be estimated using a single unit of measure, for example, only minutes/ only hours/ only days/ only weeks/ only months, etc. Some programs allow only whole (integer) number estimates, while others allow decimal estimates (1.2 weeks). The units selected must be appropriate for the nature and duration of the overall project. For example, it would be less than appropriate to estimate a ten-year program in hours, and it would be equally foolhardy to use only whole week values to do a detailed thirty-day schedule. Some existing computer scheduling packages, however, contain such limitations.

Identifying the Critical Path

Perhaps *the* most important aspect of network planning is the ability to perform critical path analysis. Using a disciplined approach to develop the logic in a network, and then carefully adding time durations to the tasks, will pay dividends as we approach the next step, which is the identification and analysis of the critical path. To properly consider the concept of critical path identification and analysis one must first understand two important definitions, and how they relate to each other: the "critical path" and the "critical path method."

First, "The critical path is simply the longest path through the network in terms of the amount of time the entire project will take."[1] It is that sequence of tasks, the path of tasks for which a single unit of time delay (a day, a week, a month) will cause an equivalent delay in the final completion of the project.

Second, the Critical Path Method (CPM) is both the scheduling technique we mentioned earlier (sometimes called ADM or

[1]James A. F. Stoner, *Management*, (Englewood Cliffs, New Jersey: Prentice-Hall, Inc., 1978), page 639.

IJ networks), and the methodology which makes analytical use of information regarding the critical path and the other sequential paths through the network. Detailed knowledge of the critical path is needed to establish the project schedule, to help in the intelligent allocation of resources, and to assist in the successful management of the project.

The simplest method used to determine the critical path in a project network is to add time durations of all of the activities in each of the possible paths contained in a project network. The longest of these paths (the one with the greatest time duration) is the critical path for the project. While it is relatively simple to identify the single critical path, identifying all the other sequential paths through the network may not be so simple. However, knowledge of all paths is needed to perform a full analysis of the network. Often the shortening of the (initial) critical path will result in some other path becoming the (new) critical path, and so forth. A full understanding of all paths through a network is required to carry out a complete analysis.

Using the same logic from the ADM diagram shown earlier in Figure 7-1, we have now added time values for each of the activities portrayed (see Figure 8-1). While there are three distinct sequential paths through the network (containing 19, 22, and 25 time units), the one which we will be concerned with initially is the longest path, i.e., the "critical path" of 25 time units. Any unforeseen time delays along that sequential path will cause a corresponding delay in the completion of the total project. Critical paths (and near-critical paths) must be watched closely.

(Note: while the example shown in Figure 8-1 is that of an ADM network, the principles of critical path analysis appy to all network forms, whether they be ADM, IJ, PDM, PERT, or whatever.)

Another useful method, and one that reduces the risk of not identifying all sequential network paths, also provides a great deal of important critical path information. This second method determines the earliest time and latest time that each

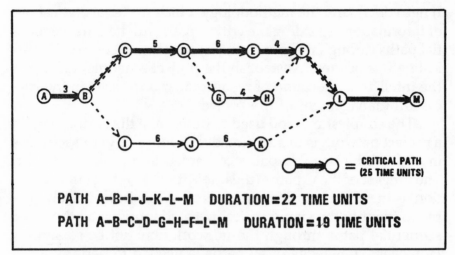

PATH A–B–I–J–K–L–M   DURATION = 22 TIME UNITS

PATH A–B–C–D–G–H–F–L–M   DURATION = 19 TIME UNITS

FIGURE 8-1 ESTABLISHING THE "CRITICAL PATH"*

activity/task can be done without having an adverse impact on the total project duration. By using this approach, you are able to assess the impact of a delay in any activity completion. We will now explain the calculation of the earliest and latest times.

Establishing "Earliest Times"

First we will determine the earliest time that each activity listed in the network can be accomplished. This is done by beginning at the first node in the network and calculating the point at which each of the subsequent activities, constrained by that first event, can begin. In ADM networks the activity duration is added to the preceding event's earliest date to determine the succeeding event's earliest date. In PDM networks each activity node has its own start and completion date. See Figure 8-2 for an example of a PDM activity node.

For simplicity, these span calculations are typically made in "project duration dates." This means that they are based on

*All charts in this chapter courtesy of Humphreys & Associates, Inc.

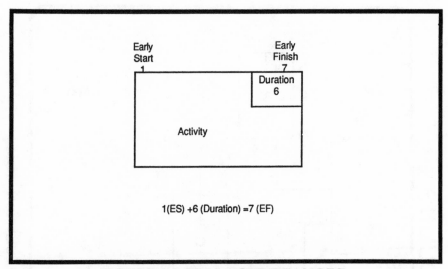

FIGURE 8-2 PDM ACTIVITY NODE

spans expressed in units of working time. For example, a seven-day time estimate would represent a task that would start on a Monday, run for the five working days in that week, and be finished on Tuesday of the following week. This approach eliminates consideration of weekends, holidays, and all other non-working days. The consideration of the calendar date on which each activity will begin and end is typically left to the "project calendar." The conversion from calendar dates to a project calendar (sometimes called M-days or manufacturing dates in production environments) will be discussed at the end of this chapter.

In Figure 8-2, the activity duration (6 time units) shown in the upper right corner of the node is added to the first start date (day 1) to determine the earliest complete date (day 7). This calculation determines the earliest date that the particular event can occur, since the calculations are based on the network start date and the logical relationships from start to finish. This calculation must be repeated for each of the succeeding activities in all of the various paths through the network. See Figure 8-3 for an example of a "forward pass" calculation through

PROJECT SCHEDULING

FORWARD PASS

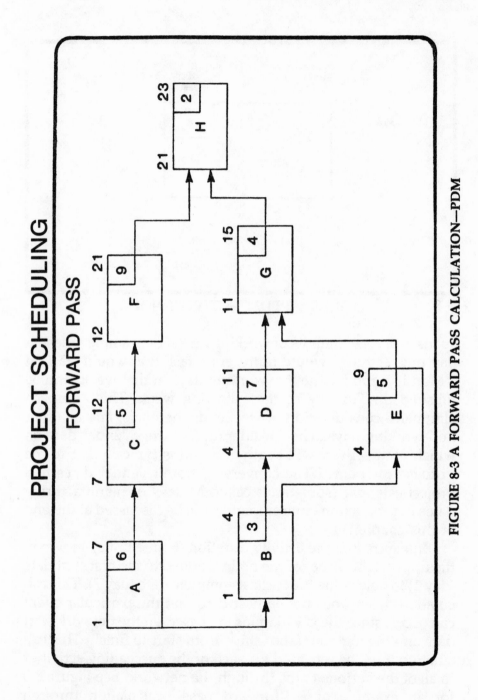

FIGURE 8-3 A FORWARD PASS CALCULATION—PDM

a PDM network using the critical path method.

The formula for setting the earliest time for a given activity is:

EF (Early Finish) = ES (Early Start) + DU (Duration)

Since dates, either calendar dates or duration dates, should represent a full work (typically eight-hour) day, and since the assignment of a date to an event is required in ADM, or the start or end of an activity in PDM, consideration must be given as to what time of day the ES and EF represent. These uncertainties are enough to cause significant distortions when using the computer to automatically process data from a large network. Dates listed on the networks could represent the "start of the day," or the "end of the day," or starting dates could represent the "start of the day" and completions the "end of the day." Such rules must be spelled out before making the calculations, particularly when more than one person will be involved in the processing of the data. Each available computer program uses one (or gives a choice) of these methods of relating duration to the time unit.

There is one condition that occurs in the forward pass calculation that must be explained. When multiple activity paths converge, a choice must be made as to what constitutes the early start (ES) date for the subsequent activity. In the forward pass, the early start (ES) date for the next activity must be the latest of the calculated dates from each of the converging activity nodes. This is only logical, since the subsequent activity node must wait for the last of the dependent activities to complete (see Figure 8-4). Node "D" must wait for the last early finish (EF) date of node "C" (July 2) to start. This forward pass calculation is used to develop the earliest date for every activity node start and complete time in the network.

The formula for the early start (ES) of an activity following a convergence of activities in the network is:

LEF (Latest Early Finish of preceding activities)
= ES (Early Start of subsequent activities)

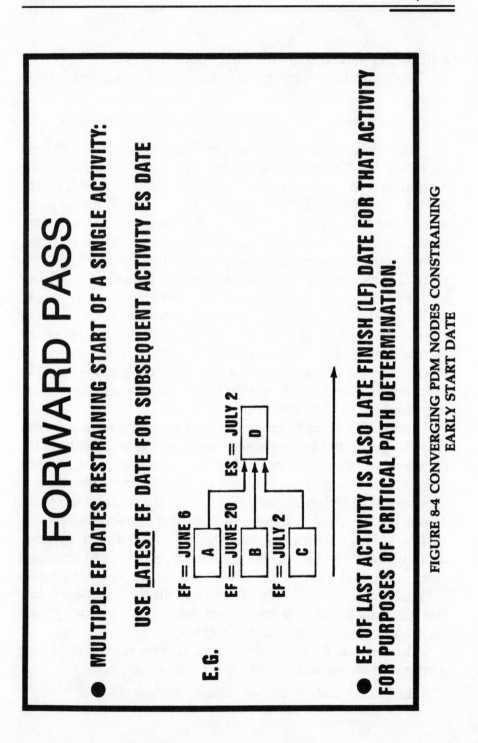

FORWARD PASS

- **MULTIPLE EF DATES RESTRAINING START OF A SINGLE ACTIVITY:**

  USE LATEST EF DATE FOR SUBSEQUENT ACTIVITY ES DATE

  E.G.

  EF = JUNE 6   [A]

  EF = JUNE 20   [B]   ES = JULY 2   [D]

  EF = JULY 2   [C]

- **EF OF LAST ACTIVITY IS ALSO LATE FINISH (LF) DATE FOR THAT ACTIVITY FOR PURPOSES OF CRITICAL PATH DETERMINATION.**

FIGURE 8-4 CONVERGING PDM NODES CONSTRAINING EARLY START DATE

Establishing "Latest Times"

We will now consider the opposite of the earliest time, the "latest" date that each activity can be accomplished without having an impact on the end date of the network. This combination of time points will provide a "window" within which each activity may be accomplished without effecting the overall completion of the project. These calculations must be started at the end of the network.

To do this we must first establish a target date for the completion of the last activity in the network. If a target for completion doesn't exist, or if we want to "see where it comes out," we can simply use the early finish date for the last activity in the network as the reference point. After the project's completion point is established, the duration of the last activity is subtracted from it to establish the late start of each activity in PDM (or the preceding event in ADM). Once again this process is repeated for all of the activities in the network. This is called, as you might have guessed, the "backward pass" calculation (see Figure 8-5 using a PDM network).

The formula for the late start of any activity is:
LS (Late Start) = LF (Late Finish) - DU (Duration)

In the backward pass, there is also a situation which requires careful examination. The date for the finish of an activity that precedes a diverging point in the network must be the earliest of the late starts of the succeeding activities in PDM networks (see Figure 8-6). In ADM networks the same applies to the predecessor event of diverging activities.

The formula for determining the late finish of a preceding activity at a point of divergence is:

LF (Late Finish of preceding activity)
= ELS (Earliest Late Start of succeeding activities)

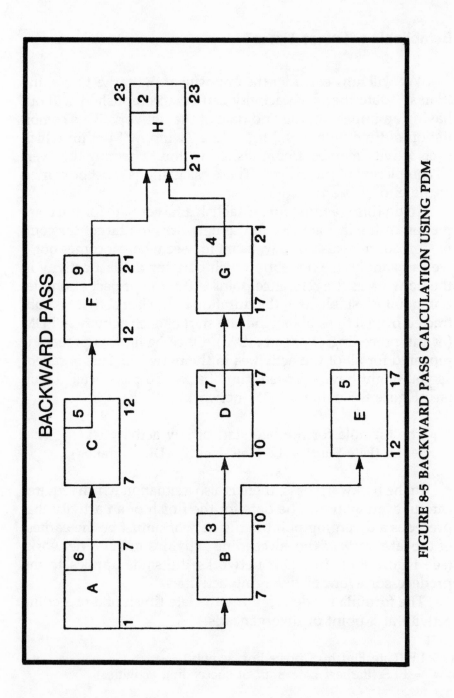

FIGURE 8-5 BACKWARD PASS CALCULATION USING PDM

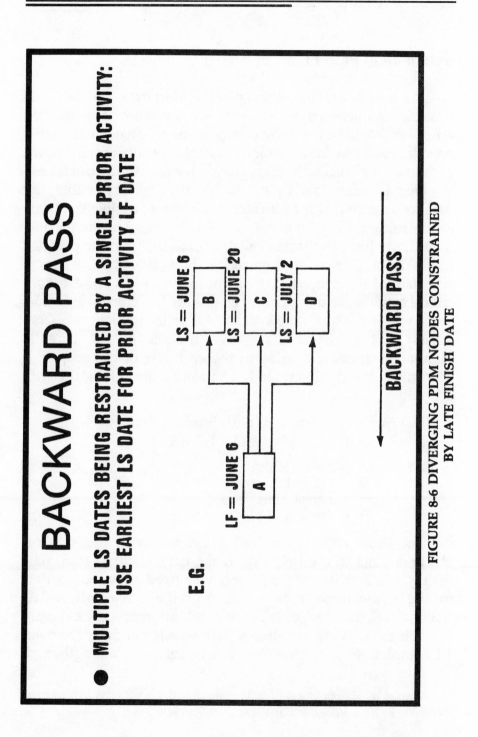

FIGURE 8-6 DIVERGING PDM NODES CONSTRAINED BY LATE FINISH DATE

Determining Path Float (or Slack)

We now know the earliest possible start date, and the latest possible completion date, for every activity in the network. This information can be used to determine the relative critical (time) need for each task in the project. The relative criticality is known as "float" or "slack," synonymous terms for our purposes.

Float is determined by subtracting the earliest possible start date for an activity (or event) from the latest possible start date for the same activity (or event). If the result has a positive value, the activity has extra time available (in addition to the planned task's duration) that can be used without affecting the overall end date of the project. Stated another way: "...these non-critical activities and noncritical chains are therefore able to float about within the total time available for their completion."[2] Conversely, if the answer is negative, the activity (as currently planned) will cause a delay in the end date of the project. It is possible, but not likely, to have positive float along the critical path.

The formula for determining float or slack is:
$$\text{Float (Slack)} = \text{LF} - \text{EF} = \text{LS} - \text{ES}$$

Where: LF = Latest Finish
       EF = Earliest Finish
       LS = Latest Start
       ES = Earliest Start

The most critical activities are those with the smallest algebraic float in the network. If the earliest completion date for the last activity of the project was used as the latest date for the backward pass, the activities on the critical path will all have zero float. This confirms one definition of a critical path, that it is the sequential network path which will delay the overall completion of the project if it is delayed or lengthened.

[2]Daniel W. Halpin and Ronald W. Woodhead, *Construction Management*, (New York: John Wiley & Sons, Inc., 1980), page 318.

Therefore, the less critical (not on the critical path) that a given activity is, the greater the positive value of its float.

Float must be shared by all of the activities on a given path (or subpath). If the expected float is consumed earlier by one of the activities on the same path, it isn't available later to the other activities on that same path. Sometimes this float is also called "path float." We feel that the term "path float" is better than just plain "float," as it points out the shared nature of the relationship.

Path float can be either a negative or positive value. If a specific target date is used for the latest completion date of the project (for example, July 1st, 1990) rather than using the earliest calculated completion date of the last activity in the network, and if this target date is earlier than the earliest forecasted finish date, the resulting path float of the critical path will be negative. This condition indicates that the plan is not in concert with the requirements of the project.

Free Float

There is another type of float that can be determined for individual activities. It is known as "free float." Free float refers to the float that can occur during an individual activity without effecting any other activity in the network. "...it represents the amount of time an activity can be delayed from its earliest start time to the point where it interferes with the earliest start time of its succeeding activity."[3] Not all activities have free float.

The formula for determining free float is:
Free Float (for a given activity) =
Earliest Start (of a succeeding activity) −
Earliest Finish (of that given activity)

[3]"PERT, CPM, and Other Network Techniques," by Robert W. Miller, appearing in H. B. Maynard, *Handbook of Business Administration*, (New York: McGraw-Hill Book Company, 1967), pages 17-94.

An activity with free float can be delayed or extended without interfering with any other activity. Free float equals the late completion date for a given activity subtracted from the early start date for the succeeding activity. Useful free float typically relates to activities that are on a path by themselves. This formula also assigns free float to the last activity on every path which has positive path float. Free float is only useful and truly available when all of the previous activities have been accomplished. From a practical point of view, free float is only useful when the activity can actually be considered independent of the other activities of the network. Therefore, the use of the formula only identifies those activities with potential free float. As will be seen later, free float is a very useful planning tool in the allocation of requested resources and can be used extensively in the "leveling" of resources.

An illustration of free float is given in Figure 8-7. Activity "G-H" has a free float of 6 time units. It has a span of 4 time units which can float either way along the 10 time unit span (DF) without impacting the project completion date of "M."

Secondary Float

"Secondary float" is similar to path float, except that it is calculated toward an intermediate event or activity rather than the project end date. When the key event (or milestone) in the project is not the end activity of the network, secondary float is calculated to determine the critical path leading toward that key event.

Secondary float is path float leading toward a specifically chosen event or activity. Those portions of the network that lead toward the key event are treated as though the key event is the end of the network, and the path float is calculated accordingly. Secondary float is often used to evaluate the critical position of activities that lead to a contractually significant milestone, e.g., events that represent incentive or award fee payments.

PROJECT SCHEDULING

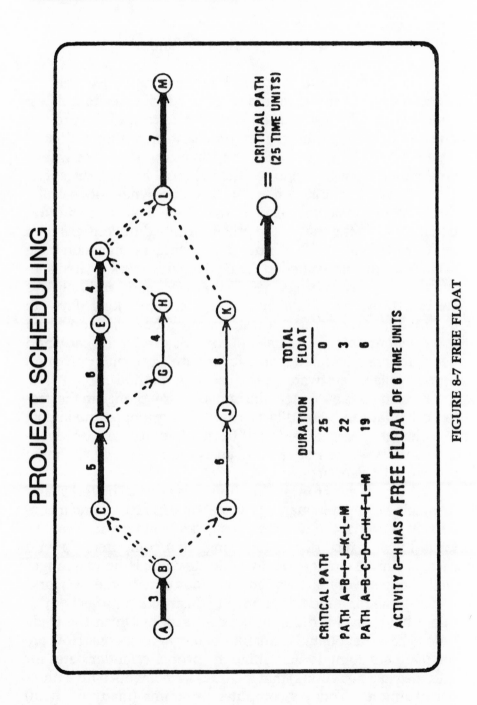

	DURATION	TOTAL FLOAT
CRITICAL PATH	25	0
PATH A–B–I–J–K–L–M	22	3
PATH A–B–C–D–G–H–F–L–M	19	6

ACTIVITY G–H HAS A **FREE FLOAT** OF **6 TIME UNITS**

FIGURE 8-7 FREE FLOAT

Establishing and Using a "Project Calendar"

In order to use the critical path method most effectively the planned task durations should relate to specific calendar dates. First, one usually assumes a planned date to start the project. This can be done arbitrarily (assume that the project will start on the first of January, 1988), or perhaps the start date will be determined from the contract, the proposal ground rules, etc. The assumed start date will be the basis for all network calculations. All of the actual calculations will be measured in duration units from the start of the project. These durations can then be converted to actual calendar dates using a conversion table such as the one illustrated in Figure 8-8, which was created specifically for a given project. Note that weekends and holidays are not shown in this calendar. Since only working days are included in the calendar, a task span can be easily converted to a calendar date. The same approach is used if the early and late dates are calculated manually or with a computer program (most available software uses this same method).

By using this approach, the impact of any change in the project calendar can be readily assessed. For example, the impact of a change (being considered) from a five- to a six- or seven-day work week can be quickly analyzed by simply changing the project calendar.

While it is easy to visualize how this approach works, and to imagine using it in manual calculations, in fact, calendar conversion is one of the most tedious tasks planners have to perform. But it is also one of the things that computers do with ease. A simple change to add or delete a single holiday might well change every subsequent calendar date in the network!

Imagine for a moment a major construction project which might have several different subcontracts in which the trade unions have negotiated different holiday agreements. How are the planners going to determine the proper calendar dates for activities in a network(s) that includes agreements with a number of unions? Today's computer programs (many of them) allow the use of more than one calendar at a time. So each activity, or activities of different resources, are calculated using different calendars.

The possibilities do not stop here. In some types of projects the timing is so critical that the schedule is determined in hours. An example might be a freeway project that involves the closure of a busy thoroughfare during nighttime hours. The activities of the various construction trades must be planned in hours to ensure that the work is done during the closure times. Various shifts (day vs. night) may plan to work a different number of hours per day. All of these various scenarios can be considered using the scheduling software available today.

Project Day	Calendar Date	Project Day	Calendar Date
1	January 04, 1988	13	January 20, 1988
2	January 05, 1988	14	January 21, 1988
3	January 06, 1988	15	January 22, 1988
4	January 07, 1988	16	January 25, 1988
5	January 08, 1988	17	January 26, 1988
6	January 11, 1988	18	January 27, 1988
7	January 12, 1988	19	January 28, 1988
8	January 13, 1988	20	January 29, 1988
9	January 14, 1988	21	February 01, 1988
10	January 15, 1988	22	February 02, 1988
11	January 18, 1988	23	February 03, 1988
12	January 19, 1988	24	February 04, 1988
		25	February 05, 1988

FIGURE 8-8 A TYPICAL "PROJECT CALENDAR"

In our next and final chapter on network scheduling we will address the management of a project using network based schedules.

Chapter 9

Network Schedules: Part 5
Managing A Project

Networks can be used to plan a project and then simply put into the archives, or they can later be used to manage the "time" dimension of an approved project. We feel that critical path analysis provides an invaluable tool for the continuous surveillance and control of a project. The methodology of critical path analysis provides the necessary framework for the close monitoring of project performance, and assesses the ability to meet a target completion date. In this chapter we will discuss certain networking approaches used to manage a project.

Who Should Own Float

The concept of float and the issue of just who should own it can be illustrated nicely by envisioning a large passenger airliner coming in for a landing at New York's JFK Airport after a twelve-hour flight from the Middle East. Several hundred miles out the pilot and the airport radio control tower start a dialogue which will eventually result in the landing of the air-plane. The task of landing the large aircraft will take only a few seconds to accomplish once on the runway, but this critical activity could (theoretically) take place within a window time span of perhaps up to a full hour, depending on available fuel, winds, etc. Thus on a long distance flight there could be as much as one full hour of float time for the safe landing of the aircraft.

Based on many factors, most extraneous to the airliner, the pilot will speed up, slow down, or continue the existing speed to eventually land the airplane within the float window available to it. Who decides this issue for the airliner and its passengers, i. e., who owns the float, in this case? It could be the airline captain or it could be the air traffic controllers.

Obviously the air traffic controllers must manage the float in such cases. Only they are aware of all critical issues: local traffic, weather, emergencies, runway conditions, etc. The air controllers must weigh all factors and decide precisely within the one-hour float window just when this aircraft can land. They cannot, should not delegate this matter to the airplane captain.

Just as with the landing of the large passenger airplane, in all cases management must control project float, and decide when it will be used by the individual tasks. Individual task managers should not be allowed to determine when float will be consumed. Too much vital information is *not* available to these task managers to indiscriminately leave such options to them, not the least of which is the availability of funds to continue the project to completion. The manager who is in a position to understand all factors of the project, and the relative importance of each task, must make these choices.

Using Float to Establish the "Baseline Schedule"

Once the network has been developed, the critical path identified, and path float established for all of the activities contained in the network, this information can be used to establish the "baseline schedule." The baseline schedule establishes target dates and time spans for the accomplishment of all individual tasks/activities in the project.

The first step in this process is the evaluation of the critical path. Since the critical path (by definition) establishes the shortest time during which the entire project can be accomplished, the makeup of this path will determine the minimum project length. If the span from start to finish of the project (based on network logic and task durations) goes beyond the target completion date, the critical path must be shortened. Possibilities for shortening the critical path include: (1) reducing the duration spans of activities along the critical path, often accomplished with the increased application of resources; (2) eliminating specific tasks which are on the critical path; and (3) changing the network's logic, often changing sequential tasks along the critical path to parallel tasks. The top of Figure 9-1 shows a network with a nine-week critical path ($3+3+3=9$).

There must be sound underlying reasons to make changes in either network logic or in activity time spans. Purely cosmetic fixes should be avoided. Once a task duration has been established, any changes to it suggest that some additional knowledge is now available which allows for shorter duration. The possibility of changes in duration spans is real. However, the arbitrary shortening of spans to make the plan "look good" resolves nothing. When the critical path has been identified and the search for a shorter path is underway, greater attention can be focused on the analysis of the critical path. In many cases this added attention brings additional facts to the surface which had not been previously considered. In Figure 9-1 the center network shows that activity B has been shortened to two weeks, thereby reducing the critical path to eight weeks. The reduction from three to two weeks might have been the result of added overtime, or more people, i.e., the addition of resources.

The other means of shortening the critical path involves changing the logic. Most changes to logic change sequential activities to overlapping or parallel activities. There are some problems related to this type of logic change. The amount of overlap,

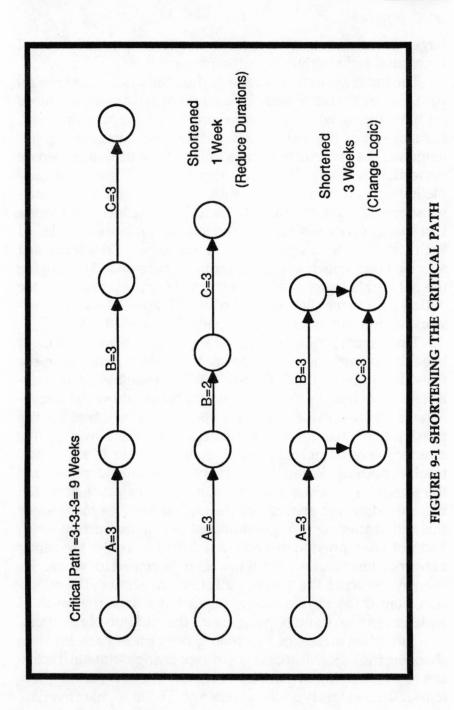

FIGURE 9-1 SHORTENING THE CRITICAL PATH

Critical Path =3+3+3= 9 Weeks

A=3   B=3   C=3

Shortened
1 Week
(Reduce Durations)

A=3   B=2   C=3

Shortened
3 Weeks
(Change Logic)

A=3   B=3   C=3

and the definition of the degree to which the preceding activity must be done to allow the following activity to commence, is most often not clearly described. Changes of this type are often planned with the amount of overlap required to resolve the length of the critical path rather than the overlap representing some real plan that can be logically explained. In Figure 9-1 the bottom network has been changed to reflect activities B and C being executed in parallel.

Other changes in the logic can be more substantial in nature. These typically represent a determined management change in the project plan. A decision to proceed into production design before all developmental testing has been finished, or to begin foundation construction before the total building structure design has been completed, are two examples of revised project planning sometimes done by management. It should be noted that such changes do involve the addition of "risk" to the project. In many industries, the press of time caused by ambitious promises, and need for increased return on the investment, have caused such methods to become the standard rather than the exception.

Most often, the resolution of the critical path length will involve more than one path. As steps are taken to shorten the original critical path, additional paths suddenly emerge as the new critical path. These new critical paths must also be shortened, and so forth.

Eventually the critical path will be established at an acceptable length. Attention can then be turned to the management of all tasks/activities contained in the project. The analysis of these tasks that must be performed centers on the determination of the "best time" to schedule their accomplishment within the performance window without affecting the target completion date. An example of this approach is illustrated in Figure 9-2, which shows (using ADM & PDM) that an activity has a window of performance possibilities ranging from Early Start (ES) on the left to Late Finish (LF) on the right.

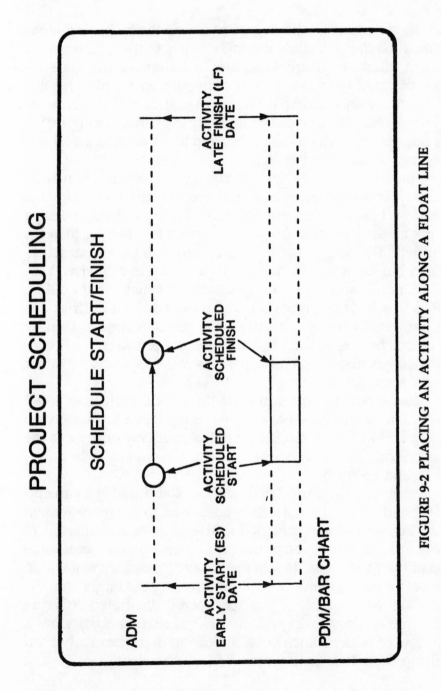

FIGURE 9-2 PLACING AN ACTIVITY ALONG A FLOAT LINE

Chart courtesy Humphreys & Associates, Inc.

Activities with free float can be delayed from their early start date by the amount of their available free float without affecting any other activity in the network. Within this range some date must be selected to schedule the activity. Activities with only path float (and no free float) must be considered with all of the activities that are on the path. If any one of these activities is delayed, all of the subsequent activities will be delayed by a like amount. Within the range of possible times for accomplishment of the activities on such a path, some date must be selected for the accomplishment of each activity.

The selection of specific times to perform various tasks/activities in the project schedule involves a number of factors. Setting aside all other considerations (particularly funding), every activity should be accomplished as early as possible. Early accomplishment allows time for the correction of any difficulties that may arise, saves any remaining time for additional uncertainties on subsequent activities, and generally costs less, since there is normally an increase in costs resulting from inflation. Also, when working toward the completion of a total job, as more of the early tasks are completed, greater management attention can then be focused on those activities which remain to be performed.

Some project managers consider the duration spans established for each of the activities as their baseline schedule authority, and others stand back and only focus on the key start/completion milestones. The effect is the same. The real purpose for creating and formally issuing a baseline schedule is to obtain a time commitment out of each of the various task/activity managers, to let them know that their performance is being closely followed, and to be prepared to take management action as needed to keep all areas on the planned path.

Resource Analysis and Leveling

Now we will look at a more involved method for dealing with resource requirements. The subject goes by several names:

Resource Planning, Resource Leveling, Capacity Analysis, and perhaps "my cup runeth over" studies.

The obvious reason to delay tasks from their earliest possible start or completion times is the shortage of, or over-commitment of, limited resources. Resource constraints that are highlighted in the network's logic help to avoid these problems. Planning for all of the possible resource constraints is not an easy job. Normally only those that are clear and obvious are included in the actual network logic. Other resource constraints can be reviewed quickly by sorting the activities according to the primary resource that will be needed, and by start date. When activities require and over-commit a specific resource (skilled people, special tools, particular machines, facilities, etc.), then something must be delayed.

The easiest activities to delay are ones with free float. If there are no paths with free float, then all paths with float must be examined. This process is done in an iterating fashion, solving one problem at a time. Each solution creates a new situation for the remaining activities in the path.

Resource analysis requires the processing of large amounts of data, and it goes without saying that the use of a computer is a must. The methods we will describe here have been incorporated in various forms in commercial software packages on the market today. These approaches are not specifically designed around any one of these software packages. Should you need computer assistance, you should use the ideas presented below to help define your own requirements, and then evaluate the various commercial software packages to determine which one best meets your unique demands.

The resource analysis that we will describe has as its purpose the comparison of the network's implied resource requirements with the organization's ability to supply these same resources in a given time frame. If we discover there is an incompatibility, or that an over-commitment has been made (more needed than are available), we have a problem that needs a solution. An illustration of a capacity problem is given in Figure 9-3.

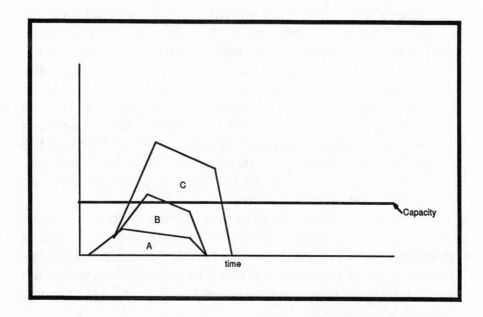

FIGURE 9-3 RESOURCE ANALYSIS: "THE PROBLEM"

Projects A, B, and C are all requesting the use of the same specific resource in the same time frame.

The most acceptable solution to the problem of resources requested in excess of capacity is to "level" the planned utilization so that requests match (or do not exceed) what is available. The least desirable solution (and the one often taken by business people in a hurry) is to buy more of the same resource. However, until it has been proven by the use of some type of resource utilization study that there is no other way to resolve the capacity problem, the purchase of additional capacity may well cause other difficulties in the future. Surplus resources, a poor return on assets employed, and some angry stockholders could well be the result of a buy now, plan later style of management.

Since the methods that we will use for the resolution are complex, time-consuming, and iterating in nature, it is not practical to analyze all possible resource types that might conceivably be used on a project. Rather, it is advisable to focus only on the more critical of the resources that are expected to be required. The concept of resource analysis assumes that the individuals planning the project can identify those resources that are required for each activity of the project. Many of the resources that will be used on a job are available in abundance. Those resources which are in abundant supply obviously do not need to be included in the study.

Commercial electric power would seem to be an "abundant" resource, at a price. However, even apparently abundant resources have availability limits. If new equipment with significant power requirements is being placed in a work area, then the "abundant" resource may become a "scarce" resource and require analysis.

The approach to resource analysis must be practical to prevent it from becoming little more than an academic exercise. This is the principal reason that the most experienced and senior individuals must be involved in the planning process, perhaps those who will eventually be responsible for managing the new project. Resources that are selected for analysis should include anything that might become a constraint because of a limitation to the project, for whatever reasons. Included are such items as personnel with special skills, tools, machinery, work space, facilities, etc. The selection and definition of the resource categories is probably one of the most important issues involved in resource analysis. For example, if a vague category of "engineers" was selected, it is likely to be too general to be of value. However, a category of "hydraulics engineers" or "stress engineers" would likely be specific enough to focus on the true requirement.

Issues to Consider in Resource Analysis

There are a number of points which need to be considered when attempting an analysis of requested and available resources. They include:

1- The use of a possible substitute resource for the one being planned (example: use machine operators instead of machinists).
2- Making changes in the quantity of available resources (example: add a second shift, a third shift, change the work schedule to seven days a week, add more machines,etc.).
3- Delaying one or more of the tasks which require the same scarce resource (example: use the limited resources in series).
4- Reexamine the requests and (possibly) revise the estimated values downward, i.e., critically review the requests.

These factors should be explored as soon as an over-commitment problem is known to exist.

The analysis must first focus on the relationship between the amount a given resource is available in any one period, and the quantity of that same resource the various projects have requested for that period. This means that if there are excessive firm demands over availability, a choice must be made: increase the resource availability, delay some of the tasks, perform the tasks earlier than planned, or some combination of each. This is the first and probably the most important of the priority rules which must be considered in the analysis of resources. Once a choice has been made between time and resources, the analysis can proceed to a more detailed level. The initial choice establishes the basis for dealing with the problems that are revealed in a comparison between available and requested resources.

If the decision is made to delay some of the activities when over-commitments are discovered, then a choice must be made as to which activity or activities to delay. With a series of logic networks in place, the first choice should be to move those activities which have free float. If there are no activities with free float, then an activity with path float should be considered. There might be a number of activities with free float, the sum of which may resolve the problem. Of course, those organizations which do not use networks to plan and manage their projects, or do not have them in place, have no means other than to guess as to which of their activities might have free float.

There are several theories regarding what constitutes the best choice. Some people prefer to base their selection on the individual size or utilization levels of resource requests. They contend that the activity with the least resources is the easiest to move into a later time frame. Others prefer to move the larger activities on the basis that it is more difficult to stop and restart large activities, and therefore they should be started at a later date, when the risks of delays will be reduced. They contend that activities with the most float have the greater flexibility. Still others argue that activities with the least float should be moved first. Their reasoning is that this approach saves the paths with the greatest float as a "cushion" against delays. Professional differences of opinion do exist.

Certain priority rules should be established for use in evaluating the various options that are available when resource conflicts are discovered. These rules are useful in deciding which activity or activities to move into a later time frame and in developing the possible "candidates" list for management's review and approval. A revised schedule developed in this manner should only be considered "tentative," merely representing possible changes that might be made. Experienced planners and other responsible individuals must consider the full ramifications of their proposed schedule changes, and receive management approval before such changes are implemented. This is particularly true if a computer is used to develop the candidates list and suggested revisions to the schedule. Computers are not yet ready to make management decisions.

Steps to Take in Resource Analysis

The methods used in conducting a resource analysis and leveling study must involve an iterative, step-by-step process. The steps should be carried out in approximately the following order:

1- Place all activities/tasks which are competing for the same scarce resource at their earliest possible start date.

2- Highlight the problem by making an overlay of the requested resource versus the availability of the same resource in a given period (as displayed in Figure 9-3).

3- Using the defined priority rules which established the ranking of all activities competing for the same resources, select the first activity to be moved to the right.

4- Move the selected activity one time period to the right.

5- Review the effect of the move to see if the problem has been resolved. Decide if the requests match the availability in the difficult time frame.

If they do not, continue the process over beginning at step 3. Keep moving activities until they are "leveled" to an acceptable level, or until no more float remains.

The process is repeated over and over until the conflicts have been resolved. See Figure 9-4 for an example of a solution to resource problems through the "leveling" of the demands of Projects A, B, and C, displayed earlier in Figure 9-3.

However, the study may also determine that a resolution cannot be made simply by the leveling of what is available. Perhaps more of the same resource must be made available to support the project. Now you know that you must add more of

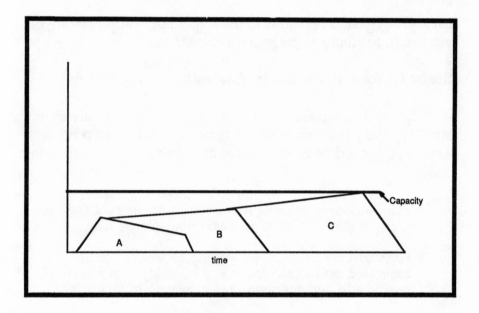

**FIGURE 9-4 RESOURCE ANALYSIS
AND LEVELING: "THE SOLUTION"**

that same commodity with a purchase, a lease, or by off-loading the effort. This exercise becomes extremely time consuming and complex when a number of different resources are applied to the same group of activities, and a number of possible situations must be resolved at the same time. A computer is required for this type of analysis. It would be futile to attempt to do it manually.

Defining and studying the available company resources works best in the near term, and becomes less accurate in later time frames. The same holds true when determining the demands for resources using network analysis. The further into the future that an activity is being planned, the greater the likelihood that early finishes or delays will change the expected outcome and invalidate the analysis. Therefore, as a general rule, meaningful resource analysis is limited to the near term. The validity of the studies decrease in quality in direct proportion to the lengths of the periods being studied. Multi-year projects should limit their specific analysis of individual resources to the current year to the greatest extent possible.

Longer term requirements are best determined using higher level summary networks and broad general categories of resources. Such broad questions as, "Do we need an additional plant?" can be addressed in this manner.

Once the resource review has been completed, the selected start and finish date can be established for each activity in the network. When this has been done, the float must be analyzed again since the determination of a delayed start gives away float for that activity and all of the remaining activities on the path. The selection of the start/finish dates for each task in the network, in effect, provides the basis for establishing the "baseline schedule" for the project, which was covered earlier.

The benefits of resource analysis and leveling are threefold. They allow an organization to: make the most efficient use of existing company resources; keep new requests for additional resources to their absolute minimum levels; and support the issuance of an achievable baseline schedule.

Monitoring Performance Against the "Baseline Schedule"

The continued utility of a baseline schedule established using the critical path method is dependent on the gathering of performance data and the comparison of this data against it. The purpose of relating actual progress to the baseline schedule is to determine how actual conditions compare with the original assumptions incorporated into the plan. It also provides a basis for forecasting new "early start" and "late completion" dates for the remaining activities/tasks in the project network, thereby creating a work-around plan that is within the target end date.

The process of gathering performance information begins with an assessment of each activity. Has the activity started? If started, has it been completed? If started but not yet finished, how much has been done, or conversely, how much remains to be done? These assessments must be made for every activity contained in the network. While it sounds like a lot of work, it may not be as time-consuming as it first would appear.

First, any completed activities need not be evaluated, and they will be progressively eliminated from the list with each update cycle. Second, only rarely will activities be started out of sequence. For the most part, only those activities which are next in a path need to be evaluated. And lastly, if the responsible managers are involved in the evaluation process, and they should be, they will immediately know which activities are in progress, and their respective status.

Many projects that are managed using the critical path method as a management tool provide responsible managers with what may be called a "turnaround report," a detailed report which lists all the activities that require progress reporting. Such reports will likely include: all currently active activities, i.e., those that have started but not yet completed; all activities which are planned to begin before the end of the next period, based on either an early start date or expected start date; and all activities that are planned to start in later periods. These reports serve both as a "work now" list for the responsible managers, and as sources of performance status information as they are "marked up" and returned (turned around).

Reporting the actual start or actual completion of individual activities is a simple process. Either it happened or it did not. However, determining the degree of progress of an ongoing activity is a bit more complicated. There are at least two approaches that can be used. One can estimate the percent complete of a given task, keeping to the original total estimate. A second approach focuses on the remaining work to do, building on the actual performance to date.

Performance information so gathered is combined with the network logic and previously estimated durations (for the remainder of the network) to forecast new "early start," "late start," and "completion" dates for all remaining activities in the network. This process assumes that all activities that have reported as being complete have finished before the "time now" status date. The remaining durations for the in-process activities are added to the "time now" date to project (or forecast) an updated completion time. Other activities of the project are forecasted using the network logic and critical path methodology. In-process activities that have been provided with a current estimate of percent complete are converted to the remaining duration. Additionally, the durations of future activities can be revised when significant new information becomes available, i.e., construction durations revised when the design is completed.

As can be expected, the new forecast dates will likely differ from the original dates, unless of course the project is exactly on schedule, which rarely ever happens. For example, if a specific activity was on the critical path and was scheduled to start two days before the time now report date, but has not yet been started, the project's end date will automatically be forecasted to occur two days later than was previously expected. A similar effect occurs when the remaining duration is greater than the difference between time now and the previously expected completion date. The reverse can also be true. If activities are started or completed earlier than previously planned, or if the remaining duration is less than the previously expected duration, then the new forecasted dates will reflect these earlier dates.

At this point in the status update you will have two sets of dates for every activity: the baseline schedule dates, and the newly forecasted dates. What do you do with this conflicting information? The currently forecasted dates should be used by the various responsible managers for resource planning. These are the dates on which the activities are most likely to occur. However, you also want to keep the original baseline dates in sight. They represent the original plan. Wherever actual progress has taken you, you still want to return to the original baseline if at all possible (or at least keep it in sight). To measure progress against plan, compare the two sets of dates, which provides a basis for taking corrective action if any is necessary. Use the current forecasted dates to plan the day-to-day activities of the remainder of the project.

The newly forecasted start/completion dates represent a revised model of the project timetable incorporating the actual results to date. The new forecast sends a clear message to management to the effect that "this is what will happen to the project unless some action is taken." If the forecast indicates an unacceptable finish date, then management has three options available: 1) work with responsible managers to find ways to shorten tasks on the critical path; 2) find a way to change the project's logic to reduce their overall duration spans; or 3) learn to live with a late target completion date. The key point is that the newly forecasted completion dates are what will happen, unless some action is taken to change the course.

Analyzing and Implementing "Project Changes"

The methods that have been presented above provide an approach to using networks as a planning and control tool for all phases of a project. These methods provide management with a set of tools, unless there are changes in the baseline. And let's not forget what that wise man said earlier about there being three certainties in life: taxes, death, and changes in the statement of work!

Just what causes changes in the work content? Often they result when the customer changes their mind. They may have found a better way. Or, the other project participants have changed the relationship (interface) between you and them. Sometimes governmental regulations are revised and affect your specific job. Many times your original premise was bad: you hit solid rock instead of soft dirt. And finally, we must admit the remote possibility that someone earlier in our path performed at less than their peak levels (i.e.,they screwed up !).

It would seem that the possibility of encountering a baseline change is ever present, particularly in the types of businesses that typically would benefit most from using networks as a planning tool. Since changes are the rule rather than the exception, any workable methodology must have a way to respond to and incorporate changes to the baseline. The concept of changes to a baseline are, of course, dependent on the meaning one places in the baseline in the first place. Whose baseline is it anyway? The answer to this question will decide such things as who can change the baseline, when it can be changed, and what will cause it to be changed.

The underlying principle of controlling a baseline is the concept that it is beneficial to measure the actual conditions against the original planned conditions to better determine future courses of action. If there is no intention by management to measure results against the original plan, then the idea of baseline control is a meaningless concept. But with the underlying baseline concept firmly in place, the type of revised conditions that cause or justify a change to the baseline are easier to define. Any time the original course changes, the baseline must also change. An example of this might be if the "legislated" project completion date of a public project is changed as a result of different funding, then the baseline completion date must also be changed. The old baseline is no longer a viable objective of the project. Variances to the original plan are no longer meaningful. By contrast, the late delivery of materials to a job site, causing a delay in construction activities, do not provide a valid reason to change a baseline. The original goals are still valid and should remain (frozen) as the goal of the project. In a contractual situation, changes to the contract's statement of work may serve as the basis of such determinations. This allows the baseline schedule to serve as a way of measuring contract performance.

Since there is an interrelationship between schedule, costs, and scope of work, which back in Chapter 1 was referred to as "The Triple Constraint," changes to the baseline in any one of these three dimensions will likely necessitate a change in the other two as well. Changes to the planning in these three dimensions must be made in a coordinated fashion. For example, when a change is directed in a contract work statement, the budget and schedule baselines must be examined for a possible impact.

Summarizing Results for Management

Certain truths in life are contradictory. The larger and more complex that a project is, the greater will be the need to use networks as a planning tool. And yet, the larger and more complex the network is, the less likely it is that management will be willing to use the network as a point of reference, or even interested in doing so. While the logic network provides an excellent detailed planning tool, it is not a good display device. The larger and more complex that the project is, the greater the variance will be between the planning and control process and its use as a utility for displays of data. These conditions point out the need to find some way to summarize results of network-based projects for management review.

The first problem to overcome is one of pure volume. Most projects that benefit from network planning are large and complex, and the results must be summarized before they can be displayed. Top summarization of network data must be done in a way which doesn't alter the detailed network logic. Grouping network activities while still maintaining the original logic is difficult at best. Activities that are alike in their logical nature and can be grouped together while maintaining the original purpose are few, because of constraints which occur in the sequence. The process that works best is to group a string of serial activities which have no constraints from the beginning of the sequence to the end. This rarely happens. Therefore, logic in the summarization suffers. Generalizations must be made about vital constraints.

The gathering or summarization of activities into a higher level grouping is called "hammocking," as the results graphically resemble a hammock when displayed. While it is possible to summarize activities, it is usually not possible to summarize some of the constraints between activities.

The other related problem which needs attention is the issue of displaying data for management. Many managers don't have the inclination or patience to understand the network, even if it is presented to them in summary form. Such managers may accept and support the intellectual concept of using the network, but won't take the time to personally examine the logic. Therefore, the results of any analysis must be converted into a more easily understood format. While bar charts and milestone displays are not as useful for planning as are networks, they do make for better displays. Combining the like tasks of a network into single bars of a Gantt-type chart is a form of hammocking. The ambiguous interrelationships of tasks in the Gantt charts, which were described in an earlier chapter, actually improve their utility for management presentations. Picking the significant events from the network for milestone displays is even simpler, especially if the milestones were identified in the process of developing the network in the first place.

Figure 9-5 illustrates the concept of summarization of network detail for management presentation. Networks, true representative networks, must contain a lot of detail, or they are not effective as a project planning tool. Complete networks might include hundreds or even thousands of separate nodes.

Moving from the bottom of Figure 9-5 upwards we see the lowest subnetwork of "E to D," which may be incorporated into a higher network of "C to D," which in turn can become a part of the "A to B" network. "A to B" can be hammocked into simply an "AB" display, which may be converted into a Gantt activity bar of "Design Building" for management presentation. Each higher summarization represents a hammock of a lower detail network.

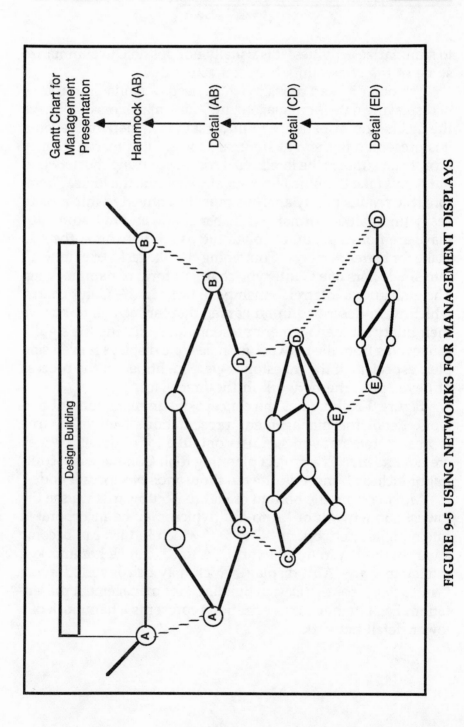

FIGURE 9-5 USING NETWORKS FOR MANAGEMENT DISPLAYS

Conclusions

We have now completed a major subject of our book, the use of networks in the scheduling process. We began by providing a brief overview of the most popular types of networks in use. You should now understand that the term PERT does not stand for "Programs Eventually Resolve Themselves," and also that when people say they are using "PERT" they really mean they are using some particular variety of the critical path method.

But the important message we have tried to convey is that network planning and analysis is more viable today than it was when the concept was first introduced some twenty-five or so years ago, as a result of advances in computer technology. The concept provides an assortment of tools for the planning and management of one-time-only jobs (not so good for repetitive work, the subject of our next two chapters).

Networks are great for planning and analysis, but not for presentations. For presentations the network data should be converted into a more traditional form, the Gantt or milestone display.

Lastly, while the arrow diagram method was the original and most widely used network type, today the newer and younger folks seem to be gravitating in the direction of precedence diagrams.

Chapter 10

Scheduling Repetitive Activity: Part 1 Production Schedules

"There comes a time in the life of every project when it becomes necessary to shoot the @!#*ing engineers and begin production."
An anonymous manufacturing manager

The Purpose of Production Scheduling

When people hear the word "schedule" they often (and without realizing it) have in mind one-time-only type schedules. For example, getting to today's baseball game on time, building a new house this year, or taking our vacation to Europe next summer. They subconsciously picture a one-time-only task (or activity) and the effort leading up to it. This is only natural since most of the really "exciting" things we do in life are one-time-only jobs.

But there is another form of scheduling which is vital to certain types of businesses. This is the efficient scheduling of the same task over and over and over again. This is called "repetitive" or "production" scheduling. Thus when an electronics firm plans a production run of perhaps 100,000 units of the same component, they will be scheduling a repetitive activity, which is the subject of this chapter.

Repetitive scheduling is a highly specialized methodology which makes the art of scheduling almost a science. What we will cover herein is a broad overview of the subject, placing it in perspective with the other more commonly used approaches to scheduling.

The act of planning and developing a schedule for activities that occur over and over is basically similar to the type of project scheduling that has been discussed in previous chapters. However, there are some significant differences which must be understood. The type of efforts that we will cover under the title of "repetitive scheduling" are those which are typical of a manufacturing facility involved in the volume production of a product, the same product that might have been developed using the project planning and scheduling methods covered earlier.

A schedule plan for performing the manufacture of fifty airplanes is vastly different from the schedule plan that was needed to design and develop that same airplane. During the development period the problem was one of conducting the one-time (nonrecurring) effort of designing, testing, and evaluating the product. The focus was on maintaining options, and allowing flexibility against the chance that the design might need to be changed (e.g. test failure) and a recovery plan would have to be put in place. However, once the design has become relatively stable, testing successfully concluded, and manufacturing methods chosen, the attention now must shift to developing the manufacturing processes, using a plan which maximizes the efficient utilization of all assets needed in these repetitive activities.

One of the major functions of scheduling is the planning process, which precedes the actual act of scheduling. This process of planning, or the thinking through of what one should do before attempting to do it, can provide the greatest benefit to all parties involved. This was true in the development phase and is also true in the production phase. In production scheduling, however, the planning process has more absolute constraints and set parameters to guide it. The number of articles to make is typically defined, delivery dates are generally set, and the process will take place within the known and existing capabilities of the factory. Often there are shop flow-time standards which must be applied. Therefore, in production work, as compared to developmental efforts, the scheduling options are more restrictive.

The main purpose of the scheduling function in a production environment is to properly balance the resources it will take to efficiently produce the product. Said another way, the planning must avoid overloading resources at one time and underloading them at other times. "The principal function of production scheduling is to obtain a smooth, timely flow of product through the manufacturing steps...to prevent unbalanced use of time among departments and work centers, to keep labor on hand employed, and to meet established lead times."[1]

In order to plan for an efficient repetitive process, that process must be clearly understood. This means that the planning for a repetitive effort depends heavily on the ability to describe the production process. Typically, it requires that the schedule plans be prepared *after* the production process has been developed. The method of manufacture, sequence of operations, make or buy decisions, capital acquisition assumptions, assembly flow spans, and test and inspection methods must all be determined *before* the final production schedule can be issued. We are obviously talking about an iterative process.

Integration of Production Schedules

The reasons for having all schedules tie together as a single package in the developmental phase also hold true in the production phase. Setting up the anticipated schedules needed to support production in large quantities actually facilitates the planning process. Figure 10-1 is an example of a schedule tree depicting schedules in a production environment.

[1]John F. Magee and David M. Boodman, *Production Planning and Inventory Control* (New York:McGraw-Hill Book Company, 1967), page 239.

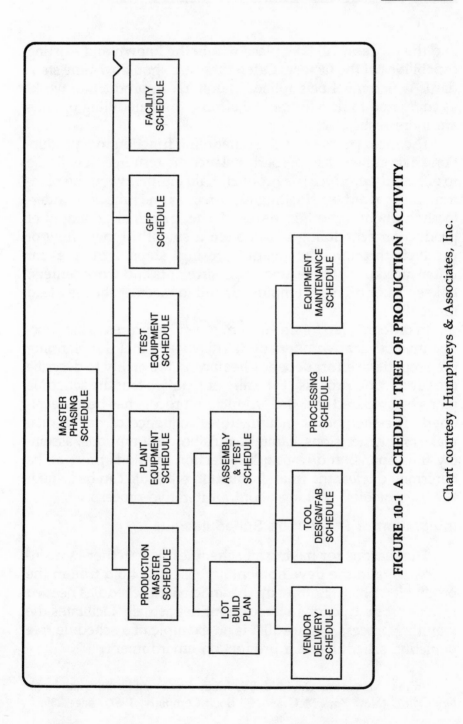

FIGURE 10-1 A SCHEDULE TREE OF PRODUCTION ACTIVITY

Chart courtesy Humphreys & Associates, Inc.

A second and necessary step in the process of scheduling for production is making sure that all the various schedules convey the same overall message. Do they plan for the same activities in the same time frames? If not, there are conflicts in the timing of tasks and someone must take action to get all organizations working to the same plan. Figure 10-2 illustrates the integration and the tracing of production schedule activities.

Type of Manufacturing Activity

Before setting out to schedule something, it is probably wise to understand the type of business one is in. This issue is particularly critical in the manufacturing industry, where the capital outlays are significant in relation to the workers employed. The two extremes of this issue in a manufacturing environment are "job shop" versus "continuous production."

In a job shop-type environment the work is performed in work centers made up around special types of machinery or operations. Work flows in small batches, and the set-up cost from one job to the next is high per article produced, in comparison to large quantity runs in a continuous production operation. The key advantage of this type of manufacturing organization is that of flexibility. They can take on additional work, transfer out jobs, work around critically needed items, and go to overtime/multiple shifts with ease, to adapt to changing manufacturing demands. Job shop operations are typically more expensive (per unit cost) than large production runs.

At the other extreme is the large, continuous production run. Here, there is a high initial investment in special-purpose machinery and tooling. The product assemblies flow in physically contiguous areas. Machine operators are less skilled and perform the same limited functions over and over. The per unit costs of labor, machine operator and non-machine processors, is comparatively low. However, in a continuous production environment, there is no room for change of direction. Once established, the run must go to the planned completion, or the

SCHEDULE INTEGRATION

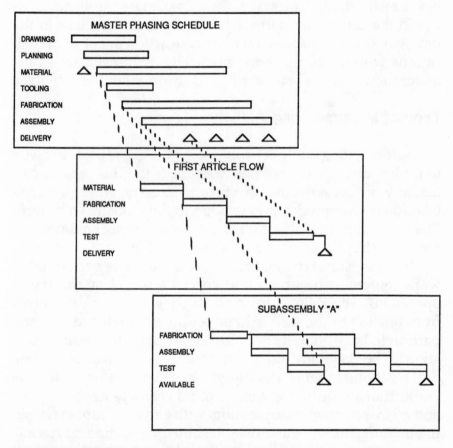

FIGURE 10-2 INTEGRATION AND TRACEABILITY OF PRODUCTION SCHEDULES

Chart courtesy Humphreys & Associates, Inc.

cost per unit goes up. There is little flexibility in the large production run.

Somewhere in the middle of these two extremes is where many manufacturing companies reside. Products to be produced are "batched" in what is referred to as "lots." Orders are combined to the greatest extent possible to reduce set-up costs, which may result in longer time spans as the initial orders are held while waiting for additional orders for the same product.

The point to be made here is that when planning and scheduling for production, it is critical that the effort being planned be consistent with the direction of the manufacturing company: job shop, lot releases, continuous production, or some combination of all three. Sometimes, because of changed economic conditions, a given manufacturing firm may have altered its product thrust and not all of its employees have heard the message. The planning and scheduling must be consistent with the strategic direction and manufacturing orientation of a firm. To be consistent, one must know the intended direction of the firm.

Standard Shop Lead Times

Many production factories have found it beneficial to develop (for their internal use) a set of standard flow times which serve as "policy" guidelines for all work being planned for their shops. Through experience, they have found that certain types of parts and assemblies (based on complexity, materials, etc.) take a set amount of time to flow through their plant, for whatever reason. Some firms go further and attempt to go into the rationale for these lead times in a very scientific way, dissecting and analyzing the various steps which cumulatively establish the flow times. Other firms simply accept the times as empirical evidence that it takes so long to do certain jobs, and let it go at that, "If it works don't fix it." These policy statements go by various titles, "Scheduling Rules," "Time Standards", etc., but all have the same purpose: schedule the entire factory by the same rules.

Those who are laying out schedules for new production work in these shops must use the standard shop lead times to plan the effort. Any deviations from these set standard times must go to senior management for prior approval, since a departure gives one job a higher (relative) priority in the same shop.

Both in theory and in practice these standard shop lead times work well in programming work through the factory. But guidelines have their exceptions:

> Every company that manufactures products uses a certain number of weeks as its "standard production lead time." This number may be anything from several weeks up to six months. Yet in every case, when an emergency arises, product can be turned out (heavily expedited) in a much shorter period—often in only a few days. It has become more widely recognized that this phenomenon exists because the actual hours required to build a product are only a fraction of its total lead time. The remainder consists of queue, or waiting time.[2]

As certain jobs start to run into problems (time wise), or customers start to demand that their products be delivered "as promised," departures from the standard lead times must be made. Orders cannot take a normal routing through the shop, losing considerable time to "queuing," or waiting for the next machine to become available. In these cases the standard times are dropped, and some type of expedited routing is initiated, but for an added cost. And, as with most departures from the rule, expedited routing can be done in various degrees: "hot," "hotter," "extremely hot," or terms to that effect.

Master Schedules

The term "master" implies a supreme something, that which is at the very top. So the term "master schedule" carries with it the suggestion that it is the top schedule, and therefore, by definition, all other schedules for that same project

[2]Paul Deis, *Production and Inventory Management in the Technological Age* (Englewood Cliffs, New Jersey:Prentice-Hall Inc., 1983), page 39.

should be subordinate to it. Wrong. In practice, in a production environment, the common usage is to have several "master" schedules in place at any given time. It becomes necessary to look for other words in the title of these master schedules to give you some clue as to which of the various, multiple master schedules they might be.

A "Program" Master Schedule is typically the top schedule which defines, in broad terms, the total program to be performed. It crosses departments and incorporates all organizational elements of the company, including the manufacturing departments. Figure 10-3 is an example of a master schedule for a given program. Once under contract, this job is to design and produce 150 articles of a product over a specified time frame. The Program Master Schedule establishes the overall spans and relative time phasing of major tasks which must be performed.

By contrast, a "Production" Master Schedule (sometimes called a Master Production Schedule) is the top schedule for a given program in the factory. It takes those sections of the Program Master Schedule which pertain to the manufacturing process and portrays them in a meaningful manner:

> In manufacturing, the statement of how many finished items are to be produced and when they are to be produced is referred to as the *master production schedule*. Once the master production schedule is determined, the production requirements for the components that make up the finished product can be scheduled and controlled by the firm.[3]

See Figure 10-4 for an example of a Production Master Schedule relating the same contract as was shown above in Figure 10-3.

Often there will be an intentional difference between the delivery dates contained in a Program Master Schedule and

[3]David R. Anderson, Dennis J. Sweeney, Thomas A. Williams, *An Introduction to Management Science—Quantitative Approaches to Decision Making*, (St. Paul, Minnesota:West Publishing Company, 1982), page 475.

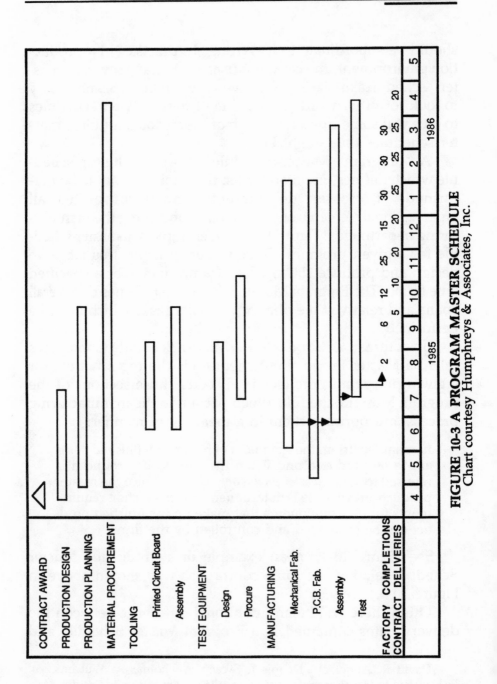

FIGURE 10-3 A PROGRAM MASTER SCHEDULE
Chart courtesy Humphreys & Associates, Inc.

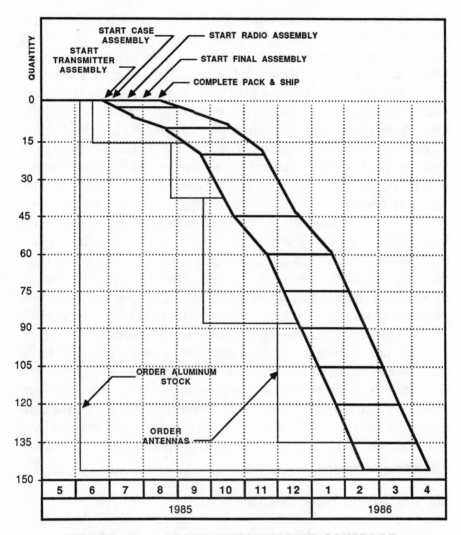

FIGURE 10-4 A PRODUCTION MASTER SCHEDULE
Chart courtesy Humphreys & Associates, Inc.

those same articles as shown in the production schedules. Contract delivery schedules (from the Program Master Schedule) must be converted into a set of internal production objectives, which may be slightly different (earlier). The difference between these two related schedules are those actions that the company must take in order to meet customer requirements within the known company manufacturing plans/capacity. If a production "safety margin" is required to protect the delivery schedule from units of product that might be rejected at the final inspection point, the internal schedule will reflect that safety margin, typically based on their history of rejections with similar type work. If a constant delivery rate is required by contract, and there will be a period when no factory output will take place (for example, year-end holidays, or a summer shutdown) then the internal factory schedules must specify a higher rate of production during the active periods to compensate for these planned shutdown periods. Figure 10-5 provides an example of this concept, illustrating a shutdown in August.

The last schedule we will mention is often referred to as the " Master Schedule," but in fact it is the Master "Delivery" Schedule. It spells out those contractual deliveries which a plant must produce to meet the delivery commitment on multiple contracts. In short, it is the extract of deliveries from several Program Master Schedules. Figure 10-6 is an example of a Master Delivery Schedule.

Manufacturing Flow Diagrams

There are a number of charts/diagrams/schedules which go by different titles, with each variation placing the emphasis on a slightly different aspect of the manufacturing process. The overall purpose of these charts is to graphically display those activities which go into the building of the final deliverable product. A typical manufacturing flow diagram for an article which takes six months to produce is shown in Figure 10-7.

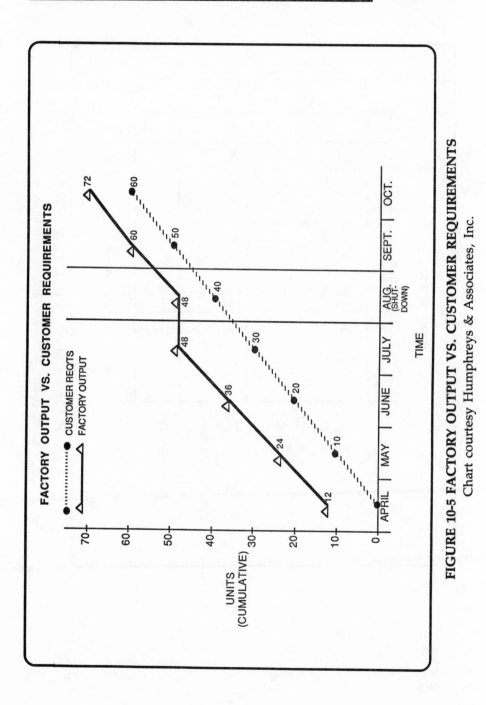

FIGURE 10-5 FACTORY OUTPUT VS. CUSTOMER REQUIREMENTS

Chart courtesy Humphreys & Associates, Inc.

MASTER SCHEDULE

	J	F	M	A	M	J	J	A	S	O
MODEL "A"										
CHG - ORIG. CONTRACT 26-001			100	100	100	105				
CONTRACT AF-0017				50	75	100	200	200	200	200
CONTRACT SPEC. "A" 26-001 SPEC.							150	100	100	100
TOTAL MODEL "A"			100	150	175	205	350	300	300	300
MODEL "B"										
CHG - "A-Z" CONTRACT 39-001.1			150	250	350	350	350	200	200	
TOTAL MODEL "B"			150	250	350	350	350	200		

TIME ➤➤➤

FIGURE 10-6 A MASTER DELIVERY SCHEDULE

Chart courtesy Humphreys & Associates, Inc.

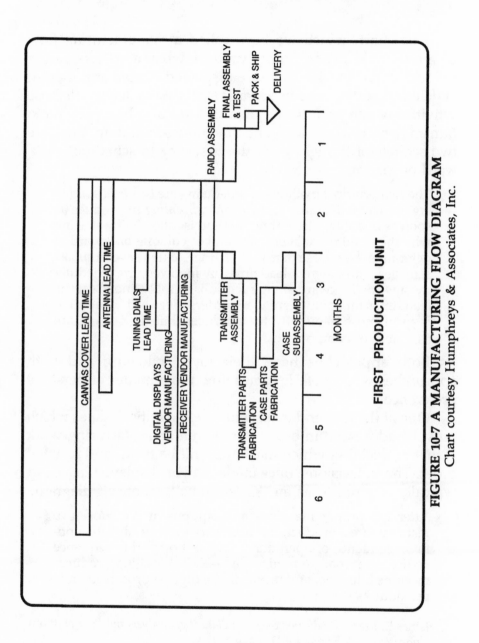

FIGURE 10-7 A MANUFACTURING FLOW DIAGRAM
Chart courtesy Humphreys & Associates, Inc.

This chart, which we have called a manufacturing flow diagram, could also be properly referred to as a manufacturing set-back chart, for the sequence displayed started at the point of delivery, and worked backwards (set back) to display all those activities which go into the manufacture of a backpack radio transmitter. As it was with one-time-only scheduling, there are two schools of thought as to the best way to schedule, backward or forward:

> The two principal methods of scheduling are *backward scheduling* to meet a deadline and *forward scheduling* to produce as soon as possible. The former method is followed by starting with the required delivery date and calculating backward to determine the release date for the order. When several subassemblies with different lead times are involved, the scheduler must work backward along each subassembly line to set the lead times for component work orders. Forward scheduling is used most frequently for products that do not require assembly of components.[4]

Both approaches have their loyal following and both approaches work well. It comes down to a matter of personal preference.

One of the first and most complex and critical issues which must be addressed in order to schedule manufacturing work is that of deciding which machines will be used, and in what order. These decisions, once made, will be displayed in a chart typically referred to as an "Operations Sequence" diagram:

> After the proper machines and equipment are chosen to manufacture a product, it is necessary to determine the optimum sequence of operations. The best operation sequence is the one that minimizes materials handling, reduces machine idle time, and results in the highest production rate per hour.[5]

[4]James L. Riggs, *Production Systems: Planning, Analysis and Control*, (New York:John Wiley & Sons, 1981), page 501.

[5]Ivan R. Vernon, Editor, *Introduction to Manufacturing Management*, (Dearborn, Michigan:American Society of Tool and Manufacturing Engineers, 1969), page 71.

Lot Release Plan

The scheduling of orders for the manufacture of items to be made in "lot" batches presents a unique set of issues to be addressed. How many units should be built per lot is a difficult question, one with far-reaching consequences. Lot orders must be scheduled so as to satisfy both the program delivery requirements on the one hand, and the requirements to support an efficient factory operation on the other. This demands that the order quantity and the order completion dates be developed keeping both the product delivery schedule and the factory loads in mind. The total quantity requirement for a given part must be considered when the plan is developed. This total requirement must include such things as the number of parts required to make the contract deliveries, assembly flow requirements, anticipated scrappage (individual parts and assemblies), and spare parts. Each unit within this forecasted total quantity has a required completion date. These dates are developed by "setting back" from the use requirement which created the quantities to be made in the first place.

The next step is to determine the actual lot sizes. A number of factors must be considered. For each lot that is fabricated, there is both a "per lot" cost and a "per unit" cost. The per lot cost includes such matters as the set up of machinery, any tooling charges (new tools or refurbishment of existing tools), the operator orientation to an unfamiliar part, and such things as material handling costs. The per unit costs include the actual costs of the labor and material used to make the item. Of course, the more units made in a given lot, the lower the per lot costs that must be allocated to each unit. This issue (alone) would suggest that the larger the lot size, the lower the cost of each unit produced.

However, since part requirements that make up the total lot are generated from needs which are from different points in time, and since a given lot must be made to satisfy the earliest time requirement, the combining of orders to make larger lot sizes results in some parts being built before they are needed. Any reduction in costs that may result from larger lot orders must be balanced against the real costs of having parts on hand before they are needed. The balancing of all costs must be considered in the determination of the proper lot size.

In some cases, the sizing of lot orders is influenced by the need to maintain factory flexibility to deal with planned requirements such as tool cycle checks, repairs to critical machinery, etc. In such cases, the lot sizes might be made smaller than they would otherwise be to avoid committing a given machine or work station for an extended period of time. This is accomplished in some companies with the scheduling of all parts needed in a selected time period. Based on the forecasted need for a given part, a lot is made up for all of the parts that will be needed in a given specific period (month, quarter, or year).

The other critical factor that must be considered in determining proper lot size is the risk of obsolescence, the possibility that a change of design may void an otherwise good part. In research and development efforts this is an ever-present possibility. The extent of the risk that a given part will no longer be usable when it is needed must be balanced against the larger lot cost savings, to determine how far ahead of need to make parts. Some of the factors which must be considered include the part's complexity, design maturity (or design stability), and shelf life. For example, a simple washer that costs a few cents to make should probably be made to satisfy the entire known requirements, while a unique machined part that is to be made from an expensive forging for a new design should be made with great care (least quantities) until the design has been proven and the chances of obsolescence minimized.

Once the lot size has been determined, the order can be scheduled. The scheduled completion date for a specific lot order is always based on the needs of the next level of assembly where the part will be used. The actual latest date for all parts can be determined by moving backwards from the final top assembly need date to the individual lot order start date, through the logical path of the manufacturing flow process. The dates determined in this manner are "latest" planned dates. From these dates the factory work load can be analyzed and adjustments made to earlier periods to balance work loads. Figure 10-8 is an example of a Lot Release Plan.

First Article Schedules

A new product will likely go through several phases before it finally goes into production. This is done to prove the feasibility of the new item, and to work out the "bugs" before a commitment is made to the expensive process of production. It is in these early phases (which are sometimes called "research and development," sometimes "full scale development") that the first articles of the product are produced. To focus attention on the manufacture of the initial unit, it is commonplace in certain industries to prepare what is referred to as a "First Article Schedule."

The purpose of the First Article Schedule is to display all of the planned initial manufacturing effort, which will start from the release of the engineering design and go through to the delivery of the first article to the customer. On the more complex new items it is not uncommon to have a series of First Article Schedules, from a top summary to lower detailed levels. Figure 10-9 is a typical First Article Schedule displaying an airframe assembly. Also shown at the top of this chart is a Program Master Schedule illustrating the traceability of tasks which exists between the two schedules.

The logic which is contained in a First Article Schedule more closely resembles a one-time-only-type chart than it does a repetitive schedule. The reason for this is that a First Article chart must focus on one-time-only tasks, in addition to those tasks that will continue on in a recurring (production) environment. There are unique features in the sequence which lead up to the completion of the first production article and do not repeat themselves (generally) after the first unit is delivered.

LOT RELEASE PLAN

LEVEL	PART NUMBER	LOT#	NET Q'TY REQ'D	SCRAP ALLOW	TOTAL LOT SIZE	RELEASE DATE	COMPLETE DATE
........7	34996	1	50	6	56	774	815
		2	69	6	75	885	933
		3	63	4	67	965	009
		4	68	0	68	034	079
			250	16	266		
........6	36296-303	1	27	2	29	825	840
		2	22	2	24	891	906
		3	25	4	29	945	959
		4	40	2	42	977	993
		5	61	2	63	017	034
		6	66	0	66	087	104
			241	12	253		

FIGURE 10-8 A LOT RELEASE PLAN
Chart courtesy Humphreys & Associates, Inc.

The most critical unique feature(s) of the First Article charts is usually "tooling." To produce the first production unit tools must be available. Tools must be designed, fabricated, installed in the assembly jigs, and calibrated before the plant is ready to build the first unit. "Without the tool's availability, the part cannot be produced, even if there is available capacity and the required material is at hand in sufficient quantity....For scheduling purposes, lack of a required tool is just as limiting as an unavailable machine."[6] Figure 10-10 is another First Article Schedule, this one emphasizing the tooling required by section.

A manufacturing flow diagram (or manufacturing set-back chart) was shown earlier in Figure 10-7. With the addition of the "tooling" logic (design, fabrication, proofing) to this chart, we would have in effect a First Article chart. Conversely, without the nonrecurring tooling logic, Figure 10-7 represents a typical production flow diagram.

[6]Paul Deis, pages 87-88.

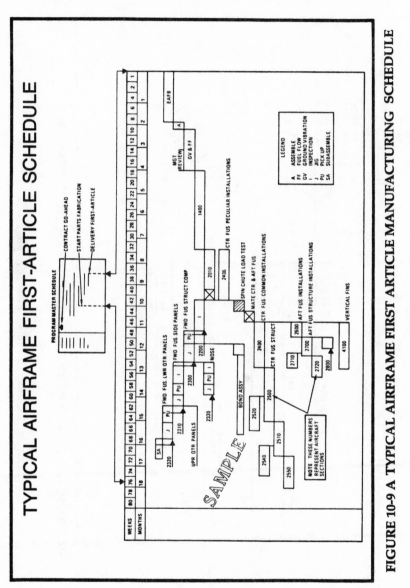

FIGURE 10-9 A TYPICAL AIRFRAME FIRST ARTICLE MANUFACTURING SCHEDULE

Source: Vince Kubilus, *A Guide To Project Planning*, (Hawthorne, California:Northrop Aircraft Division, 1980), page I-47.

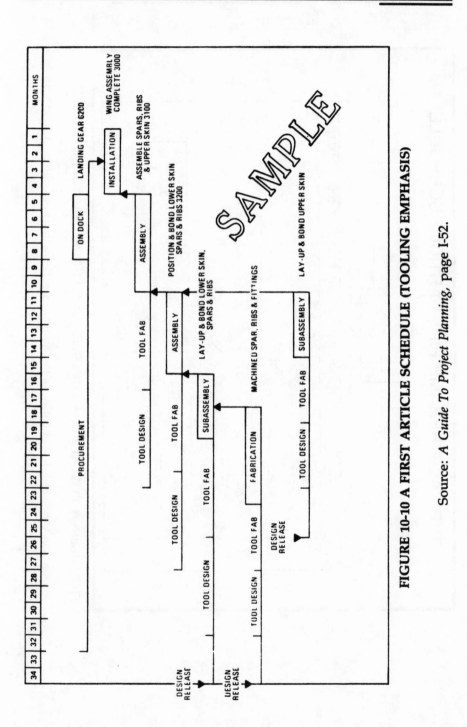

FIGURE 10-10 A FIRST ARTICLE SCHEDULE (TOOLING EMPHASIS)

Source: *A Guide To Project Planning*, page I-52.

Start-Up Sequence Schedules

There is another type of schedule which is perhaps unique to certain industries, but which could have applications in any business. This display is called a start-up sequence schedule, which fairly well describes the purpose.

In any new developmental program it is not uncommon to produce multiple units (assume six for discussion) to verify the concept. Often these articles are produced in overlapping time periods, and very often some of these six articles will have unique requirements (for example: special fatigue and or special static testing, special manufacturing processes, etc.) not found in a normal production phase. Also, there is the matter of tooling, the problem that all initial articles may have to use the same final assembly jig (for cost reasons). With only one set of final assembly tools available, the first unit must obviously vacate the jig. Perhaps a rework of tooling will be needed before the second article can be assembled in the same jig.

To focus on the conflicts between these initial first articles, a start-up sequence schedule is often prepared. This special-use schedule does nothing more than display each of the flow spans of the (six) first articles, but with special attention to any unique features of these initial units. See Figure 10- 11 for an illustration of a start-up sequence schedule. Note that units three and five have special "test equipment installations" which are accommodated on these articles, but are not shown on the other four units.

Learning Curves

Another subject which needs to be mentioned briefly when discussing production scheduling is that of learning curves, sometimes referred to as improvement curves. Although the technique is found mainly in certain industries (aircraft and electronic), the concept is viable in any manufacturing business.

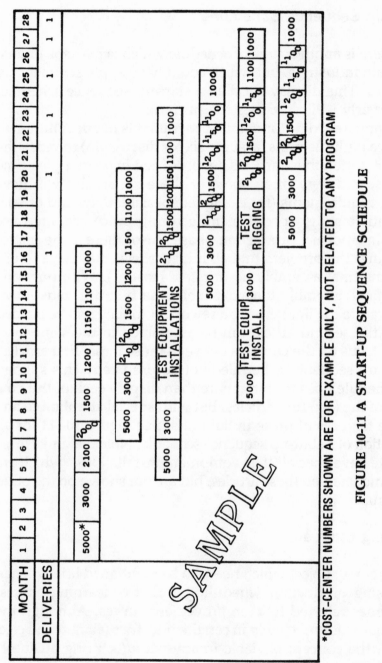

FIGURE 10-11 A START-UP SEQUENCE SCHEDULE

Source: *A Guide To Project Planning*, page I-52.

*COST–CENTER NUMBERS SHOWN ARE FOR EXAMPLE ONLY, NOT RELATED TO ANY PROGRAM

The concept makes the fundamental assumption that practice means improvement, and improvement means less cost. After the initial job is done once, each recurring time that same job is accomplished, there will be an improvement in the time (hours) needed to perform it. The learning curve improvement can be applied to either individuals or organizations. Many U.S. Government procurement agencies and private firms insist that learning curves be used to price production orders, and the subsequent negotiations center around the appropriate slope or learning improvement on the production run.

Learning curves are expressed in the amounts of hours it will take to accomplish the same work on subsequent articles. If the improvement in the time is expected to be 20%, the learning curve is said to be on an 80% slope. "Every time the production quantity *doubles*, the average amount of *direct labor* for all units produced to that point goes down to 80% of its former value. Notice that this is an average for all units and is not just the direct labor hours put into the last unit by itself."[7] There is nothing absolute about 80%, the improvement curve can be set at 95%, 60%, or any value stated as a percentage.

Most companies that use learning curves plot them on double logarithmic graph paper, which has the effect of making the curve a straight line. See Figure 10-12 for an example of a learning curve showing an 80% improvement curve.

What this concept means for those who are doing the planning and scheduling of production orders is that they must take into consideration the anticipated learning improvement on subsequent articles when establishing schedule time spans. This point is illustrated nicely if we look back at Figure 10-11, the start-up sequence schedule for six articles. Notice that article one takes 16 months to produce. However, unit number two is down to 14 months, and by unit four the schedule span is down to 12 months.

[7]Franklin G. Moore, *Manufacturing Management*, (Homewood, Illinois:Richard D. Irwin, Inc., 1969), page 22.

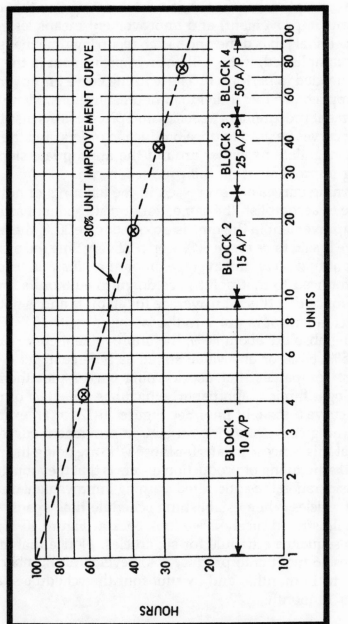

FIGURE 10-12 A LEARNING CURVE (80% SLOPE)

Figure 10-11 illustrates the point, but care must be taken when using the learning curve concept to schedule work in a shop. Sometimes other factors come into effect which invalidate the concept. For example, the learning improvements made by one group will not necessarily be experienced when a new crew (2nd shift) performs that same job, even if they are from the same department. Learning curves do not generally show the same improvements when the rate of production is on the increase. Improvements in performance come only after the rate and work force have been stabilized.

Examples of Production Master Schedules

Production Master Schedules come in various forms and it would be unfair if we concluded this discussion leaving the impression that there is a single best way to display the subject. In fact, it is not uncommon for a variety of Production Master Schedules to exist at the same time in a single organization, and the example we presented earlier in Figure 10-4 is but one example. Format in production schedules is typically decided by "that which works," and that which the scheduler personally prefers. If the message is unclear the scheduler soon gets feedback to that effect and a new schedule with a more conventional format quickly emerges.

Figure 10-13 is an example of a combined First Article Schedule and a production rate plan. Refinements can be added to the schedule when using this method, including consideration of the reduction in flow times that will result from learning curve improvements. This example includes both the first article and cumulative curves for the various key events of the process. Also included in this chart are the production delivery requirements of the customer. The stair step line represents the customer's monthly delivery requirements. The smooth curves to the left of the steps present the internal plans for the "start of assembly" and the "completion of assembly and test."

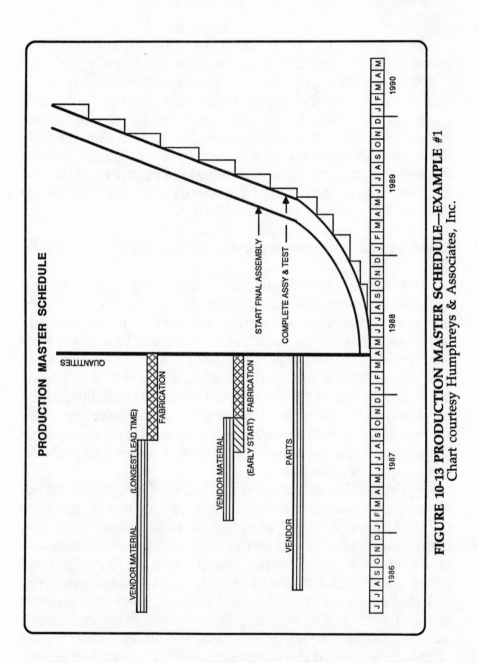

FIGURE 10-13 PRODUCTION MASTER SCHEDULE—EXAMPLE #1
Chart courtesy Humphreys & Associates, Inc.

Figure 10-14 is a similar example of a Production Master Schedule with the release blocks of "lot" fabrication spans required to support the assembly acceleration curves. The curves go upward, representing cumulative quantities.

Another example of a Production Master Schedule is shown in Figure 10-15, and notice how it resembles in form the schedule displayed earlier in Figure 10-4. These are examples of what are commonly referred to as "waterfall schedules," so named for the appearance of the rate lines which appear to flow downward, illustrating the effects of the reduction in span times. Production schedules, as can be seen, may be either ascending or descending and both approaches are correct, as long as the message is clearly conveyed.

Summary

Many of the concepts that have been introduced in this chapter are included in a technique called "Line of Balance." Line of Balance is a planning, controlling, and statusing method used primarily for repetitive tasks. This method will be covered in detail in the next chapter.

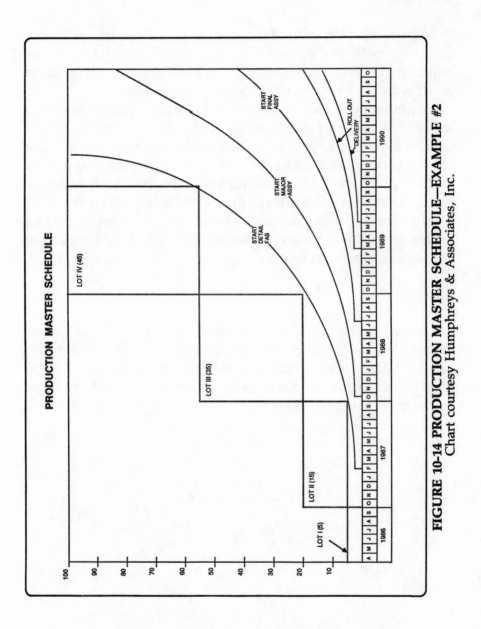

FIGURE 10-14 PRODUCTION MASTER SCHEDULE—EXAMPLE #2
Chart courtesy Humphreys & Associates, Inc.

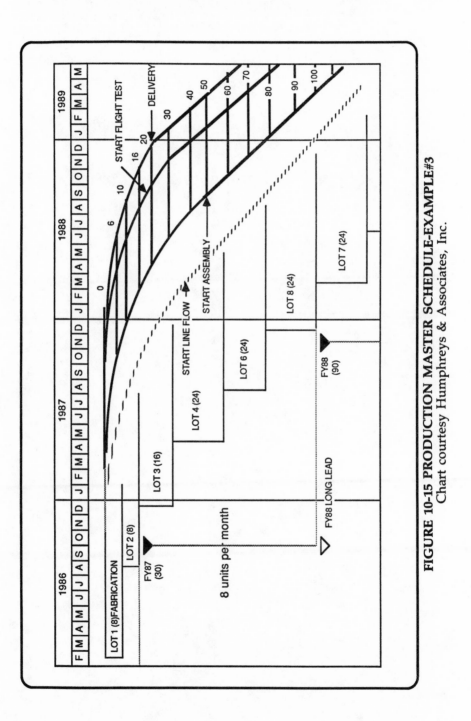

FIGURE 10-15 PRODUCTION MASTER SCHEDULE-EXAMPLE#3
Chart courtesy Humphreys & Associates, Inc.

Chapter 11

Chapter 11

Scheduling Repetitive Activity: Part 2 Line Of Balance — LOB

What Is Line of Balance (LOB)?

Line of Balance is a method of displaying a production goal, the plan to achieve that objective, and actual progress made at a point in time. It provides a type of "early warning" detector system with a way of relating (graphically) progress against a plan as of a point in time. As the U.S. Navy described LOB in their booklet on the subject:

> Line of Balance is a technique for assembling, selecting, interpreting, and presenting in graphic form the essential factors involved in a production process, from raw materials to completion of the end product, against a background of time. It is essentially a management-type tool, utilizing the principle of exception to show only the most important facts to its audience. It is a means of integrating the flow of materials and components into manufacture of end items in accordance with phased delivery requirements.[1]

[1]Department of the Navy, Office of Naval Material, *Line of Balance Technology*, (Washington, D.C., 1962), Page i.

Although the technique was developed in the defense contracting industry, there is nothing inherent in it that restricts its usage to contracting with the military. On the contrary, LOB is being applied nicely in the private sector in the management of production efforts of many types. If there is a requirement to manufacture a given quantity of a certain product, the LOB concept should be considered for possible application.

Where did LOB come from? The experts are a little fuzzy on exactly who developed LOB and when it was developed. Some say it was "developed by the Navy during World War II."[2] Others insist that it was "developed by the Navy Special Projects Office in 1951."[3] Others give credit for its origin to the Goodyear Company under the direction of a man named George E. Fouch.[4] For our purposes it probably doesn't matter. LOB has been around for about forty years and it was probably the result of some developmental effort under the direction of the U.S. Navy. The only issue one needs to be concerned with is whether or not the technique is useful on a given specific application.

Components of Line of Balance

On the surface, when viewing a Line of Balance chart for the first time, the display appears to be complicated. However, when one recognizes that the LOB display is really *three* diagrams in one, plus a drawn (jagged) line referred to as "striking the LOB," the approach can be easily understood and used. The four parts of LOB are:

1-The *Objective Display* (a cumulative curve of planned production units over time).
2-The *Production Plan Display* (a manufacturing set-back chart).

[2]James L. Riggs, *Production Systems: Planning, Analysis and Control*, (New York:John Wiley & Sons, 1981), Page 514.
[3]James J. O'Brien, *Scheduling Handbook*, (New York:McGraw-Hill Book Company, 1969), Page 246.
[4]Robert W. Miller, *Schedule, Cost and Profit Control with PERT*, (New York:McGraw-Hill Book Company, 1963), Page 17.

3-The *Progress Chart* (a comparison chart reflecting progress against the planned production effort, by individual task at a given point in time).

4-"Striking" the Line of Balance (a line drawn over the progress display which illustrates where progress should be at a point in time).

These four components need to be discussed separately.

The Objective Display

From the Production Master Schedule (covered in the last chapter), the required deliveries by time period are obtained and displayed in the form of a cumulative (units) curve over time. Actual deliveries made are also displayed in a second cumulative curve so that all differences between the objective deliveries and actual deliveries can be readily observed. See Figure 11-1 for an objective display representing a contract calling for the delivery of eighty units over a seven-month period.

As one can immediately see, this project is not going well as of the reporting period 01 May. At this point in time the plan called for the delivery of thirty units and they have only delivered fourteen actual units, sixteen down from the schedule.

Multiple contract requirements can be combined and displayed on one objective chart, as long as the end items being produced are homogenous and identical in design.

The Production Plan Display

This second element of LOB is perhaps the most critical to the study. The subject goes by various titles, even in Navy documents, which refer to it confusingly as simply "The Program." Generically, it is a manufacturing set- back chart, or a production plan, similar to the schedules displayed in Figures 10-7, 10-9, and 10-10 in the last chapter. The displays all start at the point of delivery, to the extreme right (in period zero), and work backward. This particular display is important to the LOB study, for it must accurately reflect the proposed production plan.

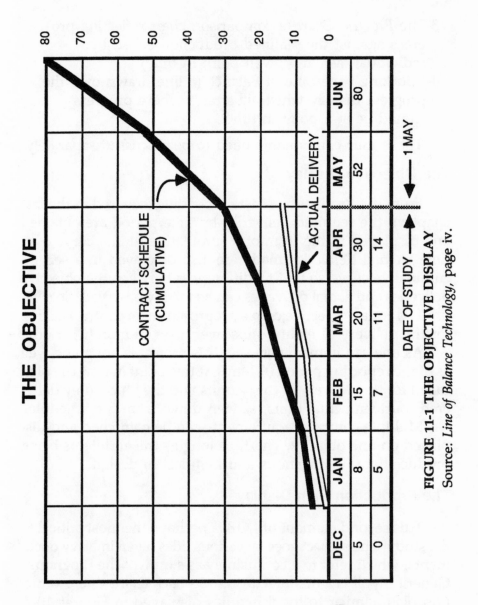

FIGURE 11-1 THE OBJECTIVE DISPLAY
Source: *Line of Balance Technology*, page iv.

There are various ways to develop a production plan and it would be foolish to imply there is one best way. However, most such plans are prepared in a three-step process. First, the "operations" to be performed must be determined. The make parts, the buy items, each must be identified and plans made accordingly. The internal shop's capability to make a certain type of product must be assessed. A comparison of the new planned order with the existing backlog of orders must be made to determine whether there is sufficient internal capacity to build the parts in the required time frame. If the internal shop is loaded then purchasing must be prepared to go to an outside vendor to supply the parts.

Once the operations to be performed are determined, the next step is to establish the proper "sequence" for these activities, which subassemblies go into which assemblies, and so forth. Typically the sequence is worked backwards from the final assembly, or shipping date.

The final step in this exercise is to establish time spans for the various manufacturing processes, purchased parts, and assemblies. This is also a critical step, for the results will determine the need dates for each of the various components in the production plan, and the summation of the times will set the overall lead time needed to produce one article.

Figure 11-2 is a production plan for an article which takes twenty-four days to produce. Purchased and company-made parts go into assemblies "A" and "B," both of which go into a "final assembly." Note that there are twelve elements to this production plan which are numbered from left to right, and this information will be displayed in the next component of LOB, the "progress chart." The number of control points will vary by job, but it is important to keep the number of items to a manageable level.

The selection of measurable milestones, or "control points," is of paramount importance to the resulting LOB analysis. While the most detailed production plan may include many activities and events, those few that will be selected for LOB analysis must

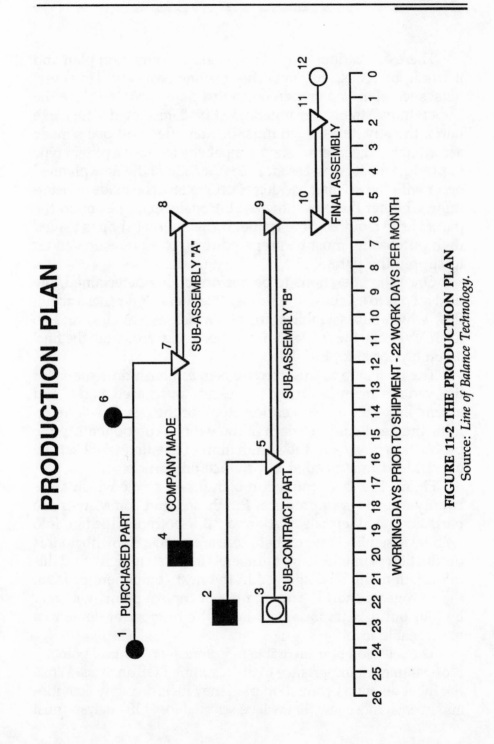

FIGURE 11-2 THE PRODUCTION PLAN
Source: *Line of Balance Technology.*

represent the "nerve endings" of the particular project being monitored. They must be carefully selected based on experience and the type of effort being planned.

The Progress Chart

This chart takes each of the control points (twelve in this example) contained in the production plan and reflects their cumulative status (as of the study date) in the form of a series of "thermometer" displays. Figure 11-3 is a Progress Chart of our hypothetical project. Items 1 through 12 on the Progress Chart correspond to the control points on the Production Plan. Thus, item 1 represents "Purchased Part," item 3 a "Subcontract Part," item 10 the "Final Assembly," and so forth.

Note on the Progress Chart that items 1 and 4 have completed sixty units as of the "as now" cutoff period, which in this example is 01 May. Other item completions are reflected by the height of the respective thermometers.

"Striking" the Line of Balance

The fourth and final step in implementing the LOB concept is to combine the three displays (Objective, Production Plan, and Progress Chart) into one summary portrayal and then "strike" a Line of Balance projection on the Progress Chart. Figure 11-4 shows the complete LOB Chart. The Line of Balance projection is a step-down line, drawn from the Production Plan activities with the greatest lead times, as displayed to the extreme left of the Progress Chart, to the final control points on the right. Its position for a particular study date represents the total quantity planned as of the final control point, plus the quantities required for the control point based on the set-back times as displayed on the Production Plan. The line steps down to the right because, at any point in time, a greater number of the initial components in the production process (e.g., #1, purchased parts) are needed earlier than the later components (e.g.,

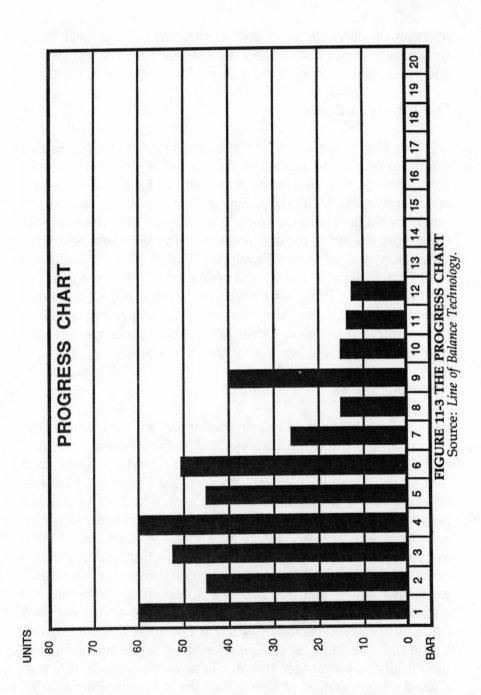

FIGURE 11-3 THE PROGRESS CHART
Source: *Line of Balance Technology.*

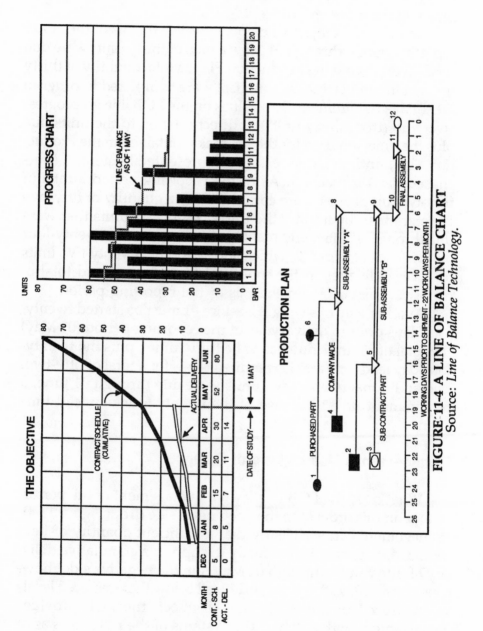

FIGURE 11-4 A LINE OF BALANCE CHART
Source: *Line of Balance Technology.*

#10, final assembly) in the flow process. Some specific examples will illustrate the concept.

Going to the Objective display, we see that as of the study reporting period through 01 May, a total of thirty units were due for delivery. From the Production Plan, a total quantity of thirty units of item #12 (final assemblies) were completed in order to satisfy this requirement. The values on the LOB line go progressively up (from thirty units) in direct relation to the units due plus the units required for the set-backs contained in the Production Plan, until the other extreme represented by item #1 (Purchased Part) is reached. As of the reporting period a total of fifty-two units of #1 were completed. The quantity of fifty-two is determined by adding the thirty completed units that were due through 01 May, and making allowance for the twenty-four day set-back of item #12, which added another twenty-two units to cover deliveries in the month of May, for a grand total of fifty-two units of #1 finished as of the reporting period.

Another way of saying it is, since #1 must be started twenty-four days prior to delivery, as of the reporting period (01 May) the total of #1 units due has to be thirty units, plus the twenty-four-day lead time articles required of #1, for a total of fifty-two. The additional twenty-two units were due through 01 June, a requirement on #1 because of the twenty-four-day lead time span.

Management's Use of Line of Balance

What does the LOB display tell management of the performance on this order? On the good news side (from Figure 11-4), management can see clearly that a sufficient quantity of item #s 1, 3, 4, 5, 6, and 9 were ready to support a cumulative delivery of thirty units through 01 May. On the negative side, however, item #s 2, 7, 8, 10, 11, and 12 fell below their required levels as measured by the LOB line. In effect, the LOB provides management with a "snap shot" status of their progress as of a given point in time.

What actions should management take to rectify their predicament? They obviously must focus corrective action on those items which the LOB display indicated were behind schedule (i.e., #s 2, 7, 8, 10, 11, and 12). The most immediate short-term corrective action should focus on item #s 8, 10, 11, and 12, to bring them up to a total of twenty-five, which is the level of item #7 and would thereby give them twenty-five deliveries, but which would still be five under the planned levels. Or, they could aggressively expand their efforts to raise *all* the late items up to the level of #2, for a total of forty-five completions, or fifteen over the planned completions. With funding constraints, which are now becoming a way of life, LOB allows management to immediately focus on those items which are completing ahead of plan, before they are needed.

The benefit of the LOB technique to management is that as of a point in time, it shows them exactly where their alternatives exist to apply extra effort, and (just as important) where *not* to apply additional effort (item #s 1, 4, and 6 as obvious examples). Without the visibility provided by LOB, all management can determine with any certainty is that only fourteen articles were delivered through 01 May, some sixteen units under schedule. Without proper visibility there could be (and often is) a tendency to accelerate corrective actions across all activities, including those areas which are already ahead of schedule (#s 1, 4, and 6). LOB focuses management's attention on their problems. The technique allows for "management by exception" in its best form.

Using LOB on "One-Time-Only" Jobs

While the Line of Balance technique was created specifically to aid in the management of recurring, or production, efforts, and most of the applications have been in that direction, there are some who feel that the concept, with slight modifications, can be adapted to aid in the management of one-time-only efforts. We should briefly touch on this concept.

The slight modification in LOB must take place in the "Objective" and "Plan" (was called Production Plan in recurring work) displays. These must be tailored to accommodate a nonrecurring or one-time-only job.

In a production mode the objective is to build a set number of the same units (in our earlier example that number was eighty). By contrast, in a developmental effort the job is to do a series of tasks only once, often somewhat in sequence or with an overlap of functions. The tasks we will use in our example for discussion will be "engineering," "drafting," purchasing," "manufacturing and assembly," and "test." Figure 11-5 illustrates a one-time job to develop the "Shadow Generator."

In the upper left corner the Objective chart has been modified to display each of these five functions and reflect their percent complete position on the project. The percent complete position is related to the Plan display shown in the lower right of the chart, which also has been modified from the earlier LOB Production Plan. Note that in this developmental job the time scales on both the Objective and the Plan displays are the same. In the production LOB the Production Plan relates to time periods, not a calendar, so it could be related over and over with subsequent deliveries. In our one-time-only Shadow Generator project both the Plan and the Objective must be accomplished in the same forty-eight-week period.

The Progress chart in the Shadow Generator project reflects the functional elements of the Plan, using the same type of thermometer displays as in LOB production charts. A separate Line of Balance must be struck for each of the five functions being monitored. In the display shown in Figure 11-5 the status of the project is reflected as of the thirtieth week of the effort. As of that time engineering should have been 100% complete, and it was. However, both purchasing and drafting are falling behind the plan for their respective tasks.

There is not a wide industry acceptance of the use of LOB to help manage one-time-only jobs. Most nonrecurring projects are time managed using the other scheduling techniques

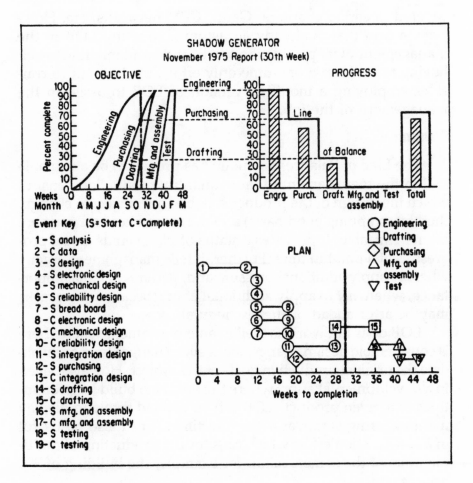

FIGURE 11-5 LOB ON A ONE-TIME PROJECT

Source: Victor G. Hajek, *Management of Engineering Projects*, (New York: McGraw-Hill Book Company, 1977). Used with permission of the publisher.

covered in earlier chapters: Gantt, CPM networks, etc. However, a firm that is already accustomed to using LOB in the management of its production work, and suddenly finds itself having to perform a one-time-only effort, might want to consider employing a modified version of LOB to assist in the management of the job.

Summary

The Line of Balance technique has proven to be a valuable tool in the management of large-quantity production runs, in which the design of the product is stable (not subject to change, thereby scrapping good parts) and the assemblies and parts are interchangeable. It provides a status of plan versus actual progress as of a point in time. Further, it tells management exactly where to apply additional pressure and, perhaps of equal importance, where *not* to apply additional effort (because some tasks may be at or ahead of their schedule).

LOB does not work as well in an environment where there is considerable design change, since such changes tend to invalidate the original production goals of the project. However, even in a developmental effort where the goal is to build large quantities of a given product, LOB can be applied nicely to display manufacturing status at a point in time. It can also be useful in a construction effort which calls for the production of multiple units of the same design, for example, the building of 300 houses.

LOB can be modified and applied to one-time-only jobs, but this approach is often bypassed in favor of the more traditional methods of Gantt charts and logic networks.

As of the writing of this book there were no known microcomputer software programs for an LOB application. While the critical path network software packages are surpassing the hundred mark, and the competition among them gets more severe with each passing day, no one as yet has focused on a simple production LOB software package for personal computers. This could be an opportunity for some enterprising person.

Chapter 12

Automated Scheduling*

"Why should I buy a computer when my abacus serves me so well."
An anonymous businessman

The creation, calculation, and statusing of network schedules by manual effort, the arranging and reporting of schedule information contained therein, and the graphic portrayal of scheduling results can be a tedious, time-consuming, expensive, and often error-prone experience. Perhaps because of this many organizations have chosen to simply ignore the dynamic nature of time and schedule management. Some firms have never utilized formal, in-depth network scheduling. Fortunately for all firms, help is now available in the form of a wide variety of automated scheduling software packages.

In this chapter, we will explore some of the scheduling functions which have a potential for automation, the primary reasons for using computerized scheduling packages, and the various types of automated scheduling systems available. While specific software will not be evaluated (packages tend to change from year to year, and evaluations should be based on specific user needs anyway), methods used to review and select packages will be explored and the sources of information available

*The majority of the technical content of this chapter was provided by Robert "Joe" Dempster of Humphreys & Associates.

on software discussed. No attempt will be made to recommend packages, rather, the emphasis will be on making the reader familiar with the types of criteria that should be considered during the selection process.

A discussion of the automation of scheduling functions would be incomplete without consideration of the staffing and organizational impacts. Staffing patterns will almost always change and, especially in large organizations, the location and operation of support personnel is an issue of great importance. This subject will be discussed at the close of the chapter.

SCHEDULING FUNCTIONS WITH AUTOMATION POTENTIAL

Network Creation and Calculation

The list of functions with potential for automation is very much a list of the subjects in this book. First, a professional scheduler will want a way to quickly create and calculate dates and float for a network using activity listings, durations, and relationships between activities. Computerized systems are extremely adept at this, finding errors such as loops, redundant activities, missing relationships, and so forth. Computerized systems are also very handy in keeping up with duration translations (e.g. hours, days, and weeks to a common measurement) and in the use of different calendars for various sets of activities.

The results of this process are activity listings, relationship keys, early and late dates, various types of float (or slack), determination of the critical path(s), and tabular and graphic reports. Systems should also accommodate such constraints as "not-earlier-than" or "not-later-than" dates, taking such times into account in the calculation of network results.

For smaller networks, these things are certainly possible without a computer. But as network sizes grow, some automation becomes a necessity. As two experts put it: "The decision whether or not to use a computer depends, in general, upon the number of activities, the number of performance reviews, and the amount of updating required for the project."[1] Their number is 100. With the arrival of inexpensive scheduling software packages, however, any size schedule can now benefit from automation.

RESOURCE LOADING, LEVELING, AND ALLOCATION

As has been clearly stressed in previous chapters, unless resources have been considered, the schedule is probably not achievable. Certainly it is not likely to be the most efficient possible. So the loading of various key resources and the checking of their profiles is an important requirement. All automated systems worthy of professional consideration provide for the loading and profiling (the graphical charting of the requirements for each resource over time) of resources.

The real value of computerized systems in the resource area, however, is in leveling, or allocation. Some systems make suggestions about how activities can be rescheduled to conform to available resources or to make more efficient use of resources. For a project network with a few thousand activities and several dozen resources, manual resource leveling, or allocation, is possible, but it certainly is not practical. Automation brings this important, indeed essential, procedure into practical use.

What-if Analysis and Simulations

Often the areas of "what-if" (or impact) analysis and simulations are lumped together as one. This is the approach used here. Both are taken to mean the manipulation of the network with changes in such factors as durations, work-weeks, resource

[1]Richard B. Chase and Nicholas J. Aquilano, *Production and Operations Management*, (Homewood, Illinois: Richard D. Irvin, Inc., 1981), page 575.

requirements and/or availability, productivity factors, directed dates, and so forth to determine their impact on the schedule as a whole and on specific activities.

Managers frequently ask the question, "Yeah, but what if...?" Managers do this because they must consider the possible impacts of their various alternative options. Managers are employed to make decisions and to stand behind the results, good or bad. And the schedulers, with their automated systems, should be able to assist in this process and to respond to management queries. Automated systems allow for quick analyses and rapid responses.

Statusing and Recalculation

Once the project is underway, things never seem to go as planned. As status is known (activities started, completed, and modified) and network contents change (activities added, deleted, or rearranged), the current network schedule should be available for assessment. Computerized systems allow for the storage and assessment of added or modified information, recalculation of the network and, as we will see in the next section, comparisons with previous periods and with the baseline schedule.

Reporting

For management, the key function with automation potential is reporting. It is the extraction, sorting, summarization, selection, and displaying of information in a manner most usable to them in decision-making. Automated systems lend themselves extremely well to this function, with both tabular and graphic output data available. Tabular reports, those produced most often by line printers, contain essentially anything required, formatted at the discretion of the user. The ability to format, extract, and rerun reports at any time are functions well suited to automation.

Graphics in the form of network diagrams, Gantt (or bar) charts, and general business charts are tedious and time consuming to produce manually, and this often results in late or out-of-date graphics. Modern automated systems can produce graphics quickly on a wide variety of output devices, including video screens, dot matrix printers, and both electrostatic and pen plotters.

Interfaces with Other Systems

One function sometimes overlooked is the interfacing of scheduling systems with other automated systems such as general ledger, payroll, labor hours, material, project estimating, and so forth. Clearly this is made easier and less error-prone with the use of an automated package.

REASONS FOR AUTOMATING SCHEDULING

Nothing in scheduling requires automation. All of it can be, and sometimes is, accomplished "by hand." But as we discussed before, this can be a painful and slow process. So it is helpful to cover some of the advantages gained by using automated systems.

Calculation and Reporting Speed

First, and perhaps foremost, automated systems speed the calculation and reporting functions. Calculations that might take several people many days to perform can be accomplished in minutes. Reports that may take many hours to produce by hand can be designed, processed, and printed in minutes or, at most, in an hour or two. This type of response is essential to most projects, and certainly welcomed by all.

Accuracy

For any scheduler who has assembled and calculated a network by hand (even small ones), the issue of accuracy looms large. And when networks grow larger and require frequent recalculation, errors are a constant plague. Computers are extremely accurate. Rarely, if ever (assuming the internal schedule algorithms are correct), will a miscalculation occur. For all practical purposes, computer calculation errors do not happen.

New Functions

Given the speed and accuracy of automated systems, time is usually available to perform functions not previously performed by the user organization. Perhaps the most important new functions involve analysis, trending, exception reporting, "what-if" (or impact) analysis, detailed statusing, and resource leveling and allocation. On a larger scale, several projects can be brought together for multi-project analysis (usually resource checks) and reporting integrated with cost, material, and labor tracking systems.

Other Reasons

Two other often mentioned reasons for using automated systems for scheduling are the requirement for scheduling discipline and the reduction of clerical effort. The lack of schedule discipline leads to out of date and inaccurate data and reports. And while clerical personnel may be reduced, overall staffing requirements may be the same, or sometimes increased due to the addition of new functions. More on this point later.

TYPES OF AUTOMATED SYSTEMS AVAILABLE

There are a wide variety of automated systems available from which the scheduler may choose, and classifying them into various types often brings waves of disagreement from software vendors. But sorting out the attributes is necessary for those wishing to select appropriate systems.

Mainframe vs. Mini vs. Micro Systems

The distinction between these types of systems is beginning to blur. Mainframe systems are those originally designed for large, expensive computers. These scheduling systems are designed for multiple users and multiple projects, and to operate in an environment where other software is also operating. Often, these computers are in the organization's home office or data center and support a central group of schedulers or provide remote processing to a field project. These systems are designed to handle large networks (up to tens of thousands of activities).

Then along came the minicomputers and scheduling systems designed to support (usually) one project. The computer was typically placed on-site with the project and in many cases dedicated to project management alone. These systems were primarily designed to handle multiple users on a single project (some, however, were multi-project systems), but sometimes lend themselves better to smaller networks (a few thousand activities or less).

Then came the ubiquitous Personal Computer (PC), especially the IBM PC and its successors, the XT and AT. So far we have identified over 100 (critical path method) scheduling packages available on the IBM PC series and compatibles alone. These systems are designed for either small networks or subnets alone, or for subnets to be integrated with networks on larger systems via a communications link.

Standard definitions are becoming vague in this area. Vendors of mainframe software are offering their packages on minis and micros. Vendors of mini system software are offering packages on mainframes and micros. Rumors are, as of this writing, that some of the micro software vendors are ''upgrading'' their packages to allow them to run on larger machines. In most respects, mainframe and mini software systems are becoming comparable in features. Most current micro software packages are typically only for small projects, and have limited features. This is rapidly changing, however, with software features expanding almost as rapidly as the micro hardware systems themselves.

Batch vs. Interactive vs. Both

Batch processing is often associated with older software systems. Transactions and report requests are keyed in and queued for processing. They are then released for processing and results are printed out (or available on-screen). In strictly "batch" systems, stored data cannot usually be accessed for inquiry or changed as the user is looking at the data. With the advent of "interactive" systems, these limitations were overcome, allowing for direct viewing and updating of data files.

But there are advantages to both types of processing. Batch is usually cheaper to process on mainframe computers, and the processing time has been greatly reduced with new, faster computers. Interactive systems, however, while often requiring more computer resources, allow for immediate viewing and updating of data, and analysis of present status and proposed changes. So some software vendors allow for both, with the user choosing the method depending on current requirements.

As might be expected, interactive systems dominate the mini and micro offerings, and the combined systems are usually found in the mainframe environment.

Integrated vs. Separately Packaged

On all types of computers, scheduling software can be found in packages which combine scheduling, cost control, graphics, and full report-writing. These are called "integrated" software systems and one price is often paid for all components. All components are made to work together as a single unit with several facets.

"Separately Packaged" software means that scheduling capabilities are sold separately from the other project management components. This allows the user to precisely select needed features. For example, a scheduling system from one vendor and a graphics package from another might be most beneficial. This may be a viable option for users who have very special requirements or want a scheduling system and, perhaps, a graphics package only. Often, however, the access languages for the various parts are different, even though specialized needs are met and the total price may be lower.

With vs. Without Computer Hardware

While many vendors sell software only and do not sell equipment, more and more vendors are combining hardware and software to offer "bundled" or "turn-key" packages. If the user already has hardware with available capacity, or plans to upgrade existing hardware, this may not be an attractive offer. There are advantages, however, in buying hardware and software from the same vendor. The primary advantage is that the user gets a dedicated machine, matched for performance with the software, delivered from one source, and with vendor support personnel trained in hardware, operating system, and scheduling software together.

EVALUATING AND SELECTING SOFTWARE PACKAGES

Before evaluating and selecting scheduling software, the organization's scheduling requirements must first be defined, even if the selection is only from two or three choices and the amount of money is relatively small. This statement often elicits two types of off-the-cuff responses: "The packages we're looking at are very popular, they're bound to meet any needs we might come up with" and "We're only spending a few thousand dollars, why bother with a time-consuming and costly evaluation process.''

First, scheduling software differs from vendor to vendor. While the basic scheduling methodologies may appear to be the same, the details are often diverse. Report-writing capabilities are widely different and the way the system "presents itself" to the user will vary. Even details like how many predecessors an activity can have and how milestones are handled will differ between packages. A closer look can reveal differences that often eliminate systems from consideration or lead to subsequent costly "enhancement" programming.

Second, the cost of automating the scheduling function is never just the cost of a software package alone. Personnel have to be trained, often a corporate culture has to be changed. Procedures must be rewritten, managers must be convinced to use the results, types of output increased, etc. All of this costs not only money but the good will and momentum of the group. If the package does not meet the requirements of the organization, not only does additional money have to be spent to correct the problems (or for other packages brought in to replace the original one), but implementation is delayed, harmony and momentum lost, careers sometimes damaged, and the duration of the successful operational implementation of the scheduling software greatly increased. The total cost of a poorly selected and implemented scheduling package can be very high indeed.

The moral of this story is simple but absolute: *always* define your project management requirements *before* scheduling packages are evaluated and purchased.

General Considerations

Before getting to the details, there are certain general considerations that must be taken into account. Is the package to run on an existing computer or one to be purchased? If an existing one, what is the operating system (this may vary even on the same machine) and is there enough capacity to run a scheduling function in a timely fashion? Are linkages to existing automated systems (such as payroll, labor hours, material, project costing, etc.) required? Is an integrated or scheduling-only package desired? Will the system be required to support one project or operate in a multi-project environment? What about future considerations and growth?

Will you need interactive capability, or batch, or both? What security features are required (password control over updating, inquiry, reporting, etc.)? Will you want to purchase a system (paid-up license) or lease it for a trial period? What are your maintenance and support requirements? What about in the future? Will you have your own training and support staff or rely on the vendor?

Specific Considerations

When the general considerations are decided upon (or at least some alternatives specified), more specific scheduling considerations must be made. What networking technique (ADM, PDM) will be used? Are both methods required, depending upon the project? Will "hammocks" and "fragnets" be used? Some software systems are lacking some or most of these capabilities (you might be surprised which popular ones don't have full capability). What capacities are required for various data components and what coding schemes are needed to satisfy existing or desired procedures (for example: numeric or alphanumeric activity codes), and for how long? Will a summarization procedure be required to produce schedules at different levels from a single network? What about calendars? How many will be needed and what are their required characteristics?

Are multiple schedules required, and what comparisons are needed on reports? Do you plan to status the schedule (some of the micro systems don't provide for statusing)? Will you do resource loading? How about resource leveling or allocation? What kind of resource allocation (serial or parallel)? Will "what-if" analysis or simulation be required? How firm is that requirement?

Will a general or special-purpose report writer be needed, or will you be able to function with standard reports? What graphics are needed (network, bar chart, general business, resource curves, etc.)? How will you evaluate ease of use, error checking and correction capabilities, maintenance procedures, documentation, and training materials?

Clearly, the list goes on. But the point is that each organization must determine its own needs and apply those needs in the evaluation of software package alternatives—and determine if the cost of a package is worth the extra features available.

Detail Requirements

Even beyond the specific considerations, additional details are usually necessary to adequately evaluate software packages once the process has begun. In fact, some organizations will develop extensive detail lists of requirements, covering many pages of "checklist" information. These details cover such topics as how, specifically, statusing is to be done. Can activities be completed out of sequence? Are activities assumed to be started or completed when the status dates pass, or will the activity be pushed into the future if no status is given? Can activities have remaining durations longer than the original duration? There are literally hundreds of possible requirements, many of which are unique to your situation. The listing of these requirements is not trivial, but is always rewarding when the selected product performs without surprises.

Testing Your Requirements

Regardless of the requirements you identify and the thoroughness of your research, the best way to really tell if a system is going to meet your needs is to conduct a system test. The test should preferably be conducted on your own computer, at your location, and using networks and procedures designed to emulate your actual project requirements. The network should also be (independently) manually calculated and the results and report requirements available to compare to the system test output.

You are likely to be surprised by the results. But the "hands on" use of the system under your conditions is the "acid test" for its suitability in meeting your needs. If the vendor refuses to allow you a systems test, if not at your location at least at theirs but with you doing the work, you might want to quickly eliminate that package from consideration. Some computer or software stores may be reluctant to allow such demonstrations. However, if you go directly to the vendor with your request for a test of the system, most are likely to accommodate you.

Vendor Considerations

Often overlooked in the evaluation of software is the status of the vendor. The package may look good, but can the vendor supply references? Not just any reference, but in your same industry and using the package as you plan to use it. Is there a "user group" for the package? How often do they meet and what influence does the group have on vendor enhancements to the system? Does the vendor have development plans that will impact you and how have they performed on them in the past? Does the vendor have personnel to provide support, training, and maintenance? What are the hours for support and what is the response time for training and maintenance?

Equally important are such considerations as the vendor's history in the industry, financial commitments, and any other systems being offered. Remember, if you are buying a system to use throughout your company, and for many years, you are forming a partnership with the vendor. You want to make sure they are going to be around, and in that particular business, in the foreseeable future. This is necessary for future enhancements, maintenance, training, and general support.

Requirements Documentation

One important thing you will want to do is put in writing your own requirements definition, and the results of your comparisons and tests. This document will provide the basis for a clear agreement among potential users in your own organization (people will have their favorites), supply the basis for a Request for Quote (RFQ) if one is to be sent to vendors, and will drive the evaluation and selection process as objectively as possible.

SOURCES OF INFORMATION

General Systems Information

Vendors and their representatives, of course, will supply you with brochures, systems specifications, input format and output examples, and even, in some cases, manuals and training documents. These are very valuable in determining systems features, capabilities and required procedures. But they are not likely to be enough.

The Project Management Institute (PMI), an excellent professional association with over 5,000 members worldwide, publishes a journal five times a year. The journal contains not only advertisements from the major software vendors, but often contains reviews and commentary on software packages. PMI members can also act as a sounding board for available systems and, sometimes, user referrals. In addition, PMI periodically publishes their survey of project management software. While the contents are typically responses to forms completed by vendors, and the publication has been criticized for not including all packages, it can act as a starting point for reviewing available systems.

The American Association of Cost Engineers (AACE) is also an excellent professional association which publishes its own journal. Don't be misled by the "Cost Engineer" part of the title. They get involved in many aspects of project management, including project scheduling and the integration of cost with schedule data.

Both associations hold annual conferences where members meet to share information, including software requirements and experiences, and most major software vendors display their wares.

Another document, the *Project Management Software Directory*, first published in 1985 by PMNet of Palo Alto, California, is also available. It lists software by various classifications, including type of hardware, operating system, and vendor.

If the selection of automated systems becomes a substantial task for an organization, impacting many millions of dollars in projects, and insufficient expertise is available in-house, consulting firms can be used to assist in needs assessment and system evaluation. These firms can be very beneficial in sorting out requirements and cost/benefit analyses, and usually have experience with a wide range of systems as well as basic scheduling and project management experience.

IBM PC/XT/AT Systems

The advent of the IBM PC, and its growth to professional size, has resulted in a tremendous boom in the availability of automated scheduling systems. In particular, the IBM PC/XT/AT series (and compatibles) has put the microcomputer firmly into the work place, and there are, as of this writing, over 100 project scheduling software packages available for these machines.

While the references discussed above still apply, other documents are useful in keeping track of these systems. PC World, PC Magazine, and InfoWorld (to name just three of many) are excellent magazines, containing product advertisements and system reviews. Caution: many of the reviews are written by micro-computer specialists who lack project management experience or knowledge, and are not as useful as they might otherwise be. Others are written by well known project management professionals and offer helpful advice and evaluations.

Other Micro Systems

As of this writing there are other computer systems and software available which have made valuable contributions to the advancement of scheduling. The Apple series with its Lisa and Macintosh units, and other computers which are CP/M (control program for microcomputers) based immediately come to mind. Since over 90% of the industry has made a commitment in the direction of the IBM PC/XT/AT and compatibles, and over 95% of the available scheduling software packages are focused in this same direction, we will limit our discussion to that series for the present.

STAFFING AND ORGANIZATIONAL IMPACTS

Sometimes ignored in the rush to automate is an evaluation of staffing and organizational impacts. If a large-scale system is to be used, or if the system will impact millions of dollars worth of projects and hundreds (perhaps thousands) of people, staffing requirements will probably require some change. Not only will key project management and scheduling personnel be required to understand what the software can do, but additional personnel, with a combination of project management, scheduling, and automation skills, may be needed.

This seems to contradict earlier statements about the reduction of personnel. Actually, given the same output requirements as a manual system, clerical personnel requirements do usually decrease. But the need for professionalism usually increases, primarily because of increasing system complexity and heavier use of the system (more frequent network analyses, resource allocation, "what-if" analysis, and so forth).

Often, a central group (Project Support Services perhaps) may be needed in large organizations not only to handle scheduling issues, but to train and assist users in automating their scheduling functions. This group can also serve as a focal point for a company "user group" to coordinate long range plans, provide cross-departmental assistance, and interface with the software vendors. Some companies put this group in their existing data processing departments since it uses automated systems. Others place them in the user departments. We are of the belief that the closer they are organizationally to the user of the system, the more beneficial and responsive they are likely to be.

In small organizations, or when only one project is using the system, a separate project support group is generally not required.

FUTURE DIRECTIONS

Networking Networks

One of the more exciting prospects in recent years is the concept of "networking of networks" for a given project, a series of projects, a large department, or a total firm. This approach requires "top down" performance parameters/goals to be given to the lower levels of the organization/project, with each of the lower levels then creating and maintaining their individual subordinate networks. Such networks are then integrated with "bottom up" available-date information, with any differences worked out through various iterations. As activities are statused, the results are fed upward and incorporated into higher level networks. As requirements change from above, this information is passed down for inclusion and adjustments made to the lower level networks. The day of the single, large network for a project may be coming to an end.

This approach allows lower level managers the liberty of performing their own "what-if" analyses and simulations without affecting higher level networks or results.

One of the pacing factors for this approach in the future will be the development of more powerful microcomputer hardware and software, and improvements in local area networks (LANs) and other communications methods.

Growth in Microcomputer Power

Hand in hand with the networking of networks will come further growth in the power of microcomputing hardware. It is questionable whether or not we should call them "micros" anymore, for they are quickly overtaking the capacities of the mainframes and minis of just a few years back. And of equal consequence, the costs are dropping dramatically.

The big issues will likely become the control of data and the use of prescribed procedures for the linkage of the hardware and data together. "Who" will control the data and procedures will become very important.

Software Speed and Features

Software will continue to trail developments in hardware and networking networks, but will continue to expand rapidly. Full-function scheduling and integrated project management software on smaller hardware and at a lower cost will soon begin to *exceed* the larger mainframe software package capabilities. And the processing of data, in terms of speed and efficiency, will continue to improve.

Artificial Intelligence (AI)

Plan on AI to make its debut in scheduling and other project management software in the late 1980s. But AI will probably not be viable as a management tool until the middle of the next decade. After all, basic disciplined scheduling procedures are still lacking in too many organizations today. What AI will eventually provide are such things as company experience in specific endeavors, better extrapolations of current performances into the future, and more complex error (or condition) checking in a real time environment. Look for more top-management guidance available to lower managers as they interactively review the areas for which they are responsible.

The information requirements for such systems, however, are vast and the algorithms for searching are complex and frequently specific to individual companies or even parts of a company. So don't expect AI to come quickly, easily, or without much pain and hard work.

Chapter 13

Scheduling And The Management Process

"People tend to work on easy tasks first, and postpone hard jobs until they either run out of easy work, or management gets on their ass, whichever comes first."
An anonymous management consultant

Management consultants, much like law enforcement people, tend to see a somewhat restricted view of life. Consultants don't normally get called into a business because "things are going great." On the contrary. Therefore it might be expected that they would have a somewhat cynical view of what people would do if left to their own initiative. But is that view too far distorted, that people have a natural tendency to do the easy work first and put off those harder jobs until pressed to do them? And, if so, what impact does this "natural" tendency have on meeting schedule commitments?

Years ago a young man worked on his first (developmental) contract and watched as the program manager requested that engineering prepare a list of all the high-cost/long-lead-time procurement articles. Obligingly, the engineers prepared the list and the procurement people grouped them into three broad categories: six-week, twelve-week, and twenty-week buy items. Then, to his amazement, this young man watched as the procurement specifications were released by engineering: first the six-week buy items, next the twelve-week articles, and lastly the twenty-week items. These procurement specifications were prepared and released in the exact *reverse* order of when they were needed to support the first flight! Is this story that unusual? Hardly.

Looking back, management's responsibility in the above story would seem to have been threefold:

1-to insist that a plan be prepared;
2-to set a time-table for all work (a schedule);
3-to follow up to see that everything was done as planned, and to make adjustments to the plan as necessary.

There appears to have been a breakdown somewhere in this story, in that numbers 2 and 3 did not happen as they should have happened to support the required first flight. Those twenty-week lead-time buys should have been scheduled first, then the twelve-week items, and so forth. Management needed to make it happen, but it didn't.

The Management Process—and Scheduling

How does scheduling fit into the role of management? Before we attempt to answer that question perhaps we should make sure that we all have a clear understanding of what constitutes this thing called "the management process."

While the experts don't precisely agree on what makes up the process called management, they do seem to be in general agreement. Perhaps their differences are simply semantics, a personal preference on where to place the emphasis.

Certain management theorists suggest that the process of management consists of four activities: "planning;" "organizing;" "leading;" and "controlling."[1] Others agree on these four, but add one additional task, that of "staffing."[2] Still others

[1]James A. F. Stoner, *Management*, (Englewood Cliffs, New Jersey: Prentice-Hall, Inc., 1978), page 18.

[2]Harold Koontz, Cyril O'Donnell, Heinz Weihrich, *Management—A Book of Readings*, (New York: McGraw-Hill Book Company, 1980), inside cover.

feel that there are only three management functions: to "plan;" to "execute;" and to "review."[3]

Let us place these three positions in summary to get a closer perspective:

The Functions of Management

Stoner[1]	Koontz[2]	Maynard/Barger[3]
1-Planning	1-Planning	1-Plan
2-Organizing	2-Organizing	2-Execute
3-Leading	3-Staffing	3-Review
4-Controlling	4-Leading	
	5-Controlling	

There would appear to be no discernible differences in the positions of these experts as to what constitutes the management process. All say that management must plan, all agree that their plans must be put in motion, and all state (somewhat differently) that such plans must be brought to a conclusion. Now, how does scheduling fit into this management framework?

The first task of management is to plan. On that point there is universal agreement. Planning consists of deciding on the "what," the "where," the "what with," and the "who" of future things to be done. The scheduling function adds the "when" for each of the tasks being planned. The early consideration of the time dimension facilitates the planning process by adding a constant reminder that whatever tasks are being considered, they must be accomplished in a realistic time-frame, or their resulting plans will not be viable.

But there is another and perhaps more important reason to involve the schedulers in the planning process of management. The schedulers are the "experts" in the use of network planning tools, which take the form of logic diagrams, sometimes called "critical path analysis," "arrow diagramming,"

[3]"The Managing Process", By J. P. Barger, appearing in H. B. Maynard, *Handbook of Business Administration*, (New York: McGraw-Hill Book Company, 1967), pages 1-5.

"precedence diagramming," etc. They are the experienced users of these proven facilitators of planning. While management will want to focus on the strategic "big picture," the schedulers can simulate their hypothetical thoughts in the form of network displays, which can be easily and quickly modified to accommodate changes in the assumed thrust. The schedulers will "paint" the ideas being conceived by management in their planning. More importantly, the network simulations can verify that the plans being assumed can, in fact, be achieved.

If, as the experts all seem to suggest, management's first task is to "plan," then the early utilization of the schedulers and their network planning methods will complement and facilitate them in the performance of this vital basic task.

The other management function to which scheduling has much to contribute is that of "controlling," or as some people choose to call it, "to execute" and "to review." In order to control something management needs to have some type of standard against which to measure performance. That standard can take many forms, but one of the more typical would be a schedule, which by definition displays a plan, locked into a timeframe. There are two ways to control something. The first and most obvious way is to control "everything" with equal vigor. While on the surface this may sound like a good idea, in practice the concept is a disaster. The reason: too little time. If there is one single commodity which managements everywhere have too little of, it is time. Therefore, any attempt to control an organization or project or anything in a positive and comprehensive way is likely to be a quick way to failure.

A more practical and effective way of "controlling" something is to do it on an exception basis, commonly referred to as "management by exception." One of the more beneficial features of management by exception is that it forces an organization to first prepare a plan. "Management by exception cannot occur without a plan."[4] This approach allows management to

[4]Donald P. Mackintosh, *Management by Exception: A Handbook with Forms*, Englewood Cliffs, New Jersey: Prentice-Hall, Inc., 1978), page 22.

address only those things that are not happening according to their previously established guidelines, i.e., their plan. It provides management with the ability to discern important departures from their approved plan, and to ignore those aspects of the operation which are working well.

An essential part of the control process is the taking of action, as necessary, when there is a departure from the agreed-to plan. Often the appropriate action is to replan or work around the plan, keeping the original goal in mind. Scheduling, as a function, generally takes the lead in formulating work-around plans.

The "Schedule Baseline"

Much has been said in this book about the importance of establishing and publishing and letting the world know that there is a "schedule baseline." Some people refer to it as "my stake in the ground," others as their "reference point," etc. Whatever it is called doesn't matter, the significance of what we have chosen to call the schedule baseline is that it keeps the project from losing its perspective.

Projects don't happen in the way they are planned. Things happen differently, or don't happen at all, or something goes wrong. When the original plan doesn't take place as expected, and they rarely do, a replan or recovery plan or work-around plan is generally called for. And when the current work-around plan doesn't happen as planned, a new recovery plan must be prepared, and so forth. It is not uncommon to be half-way through a complex job and be on perhaps the fifth replan.

The question here is: which of the plans should be reviewed with management to let them know how their project is doing? With an original baseline and perhaps five replans in place, the options are considerable. Our recommendation would be to relate performance status against the most current replan *and* the original "baseline schedule." That combination is generally sufficient to portray a clear understanding of performance status, without becoming overly cluttered with a display of too much data (five replans).

While there is a strong argument for setting a clear schedule baseline on one-time-only or developmental jobs (where changes are more the rule than the exception), the same case can be made for repetitive efforts. Back in our chapter on production scheduling we discussed a subject called "standard shop lead times." These standard lead times are used to relate a new manufacturing job to the "ideal" shop flow times for a given factory, in an effort to schedule all factory jobs to the same set of priority rules. Additionally, these standard flow times, if used properly, will prevent a new job from inadvertently receiving preferential scheduling treatment over existing work in the factory.

In a manufacturing environment these "standard shop lead times" are used to create the "baseline schedule" on one-time-only projects. Even if management has deliberately planned a new order to be different from its normal or standard flow times for their plant, it is still beneficial to relate performance status on a given job to both the "standard shop flow times" (manufacturing baseline schedule) *and* the approved schedule planned for this particular job.

Highly complex, long duration projects often must put in place several replans before the job is finally completed. A recognized original "schedule baseline" position allows management to understand just how far their project may have departed from the original plan, in order to better understand how much effort is still required to get to their final objective of completing the job. The larger the job, the greater the complexity, the more important it becomes to put in place a firm baseline position.

One final question needs to be addressed: *when* does one allow a "schedule baseline" to be changed? While there are no absolute rules to be applied, there are certainly general guidelines. A baseline is something that is somewhat "sacred," in the sense that the project or given job is expected to meet baseline goals, and is held accountable for achievement of such goals both to upper (internal) management and to the customer. Both are expecting final performance to meet the approved baseline.

Therefore, any changes to what upper management and/or the customer have been led to believe will happen should be done with their full knowledge and (perhaps) with their concurrence. While recovery plans, work-around plans, and replans can be put in place at will, since they are in effect internal to the management of any given job, nobody should "mess" with the "baseline schedule" without full disclosure to all interested persons.

Management Displays

Management, especially senior management, as a given species, is not necessarily rude, although they often appear to be. They are, however, over-worked, over-committed, and generally short of time—their own personal time in particular. Therefore anytime one goes before management with a message it must be clear and concise or one runs the risk of having this species act as if they were rude.

One of the most useful tools available to business for planning and scheduling a new endeavor is the logic diagram, or network. And with the recent advances made in computers of all sizes and associated project management software, these once "theoretical" tools can and should be applied at every business opportunity. They will enhance the planning process, and actually verify that a given approach can be met. Once the plans have been formulated with the aid of the logic networks, rarely should these same detailed networks be taken to management for review and approval of the plan. Networks are planning devices but are not useful as management displays.

Those methods which seem to work best as management displays are the more traditional Gantt charts, milestone charts, or some combination of both. These displays bring home the intended presentations in clear and simple ways. The point of this message is that there needs to be a sort of "buffer" between the work of detail planning/scheduling, which will likely involve hundreds to thousands of assumed network nodes, and the presentations made to management, which must be brief and concise and in summary form.

Real-Life Issues

Throughout these pages issues have been discussed as if there were absolute truths to go by. In fact, our review should be taken in the spirit in which it was intended—as statements of general guidelines which sometimes hold true, and sometimes do not. It is one thing to discuss a subject in the classroom or seminar where points are presented and discussed in a friendly atmosphere. It is quite another to go out into the business world and attempt to implement these same ideas, only to have the concepts shattered by people facing and solving practical real-life issues on a day to day empirical basis.

For example, network planning and scheduling can be an exciting way to simulate a new project, to work out the anticipated problems, and to lay out the appropriate task responsibilities before entering the period of performance. It often works and works well. But sometimes these methods run right into a hard-nosed manager who declares ''I don't need that crap to manage my program.'' Without the support of the appropriate management, such concepts cannot be put into practice. They need management's support to work, and if the critical management support is lacking, it is questionable, perhaps counterproductive, to try. Since management is ultimately held responsible for performance, the scheduler has little choice but to work within the guidelines of the people in charge. Strong urgings and strong recommendations—but only one person can ''steer'' at a time.

For example, resource analysis, allocation, reanalysis, and leveling is an exciting idea which is now made practical with the recent improvements in computer software and hardware technology. But getting one's arms around all the ingredients necessary to perform the analysis is not an easy task. All functions in a given organization must support the study in order to make the study findings valid. Management at all levels must support the concept. Higher level management must demand the results of the study in order to make it happen.

For example, Line of Balance (LOB) is a concept that has definite benefits in determining the status of production orders. But in order to make the concept work there must be a manufacturing plan prepared, and these plans are not easy to come by. Also, LOB as a technique doesn't work well unless the parts (configuration) being made are consistent, i.e., the design of the articles being produced is stable. If production units 1 through 10 are different than articles 11 to 25, which are different from 26 and on, LOB breaks down, or at the least, is made more difficult to implement.

About a hundred years ago the explorer and naturalist John Muir expounded the theory that has come to be referred to as "Muir's Law," and which seems to fit well in discussing our real-life scheduling issues. His theory in very brief terms states that changes made in one area (he was referring to nature) often have far reaching consequences in other areas not fully considered or even understood. This same concept applies to a given organization and the dynamics associated with making changes in it. Changes made in one area often result in changes in other areas to maintain overall balance in the structure.

In the opening chapter we discussed a concept called "the triple constraint." This theory holds that there are three dimensions to all project performance: cost, schedule, and technical. Much like the supporters of Muir's Law, the proponents of the triple constraint theory hold that there must be a balance in the performance of any job, and that a change in any one of the three dimensions will cause a corresponding change in one or both of the other dimensions. A Chief Executive Officer of a firm somewhat supported this theory when he causally remarked that his "most effective *cost* control system was his *schedule* control system." We agree completely with this CEO.

In Conclusion

Throughout these pages we have attempted to stress the need for applying the proper (emphasize proper) scheduling techniques to satisfy the overall objectives of a particular firm. Only the individual on-site managements can decide what is the proper application for them, and for their particular project. It is as bad a practice to over-schedule/over-control, as it is to under-schedule/under-control. A proper balance must be found to complement the goals of the organization.

But it is the personal belief of the authors that many businesses today have a tendency to "under-schedule" their organizations, compared to what is needed to satisfy the full objectives of their firms. This tendency is the result of many complex issues dealing with individuals and the experiences they have had in the past. Some may have tried the more sophisticated scheduling techniques before, some as long as twenty-five years ago, and found them to be ineffective. They have therefore stayed with the more traditional forms of scheduling, e.g., the Gantt and milestone displays. They have stayed with these traditions even after their businesses have drifted into a more complex and possibly competitive environment, which called for greater sophistication in the scheduling approach.

A brief summary may best illustrate the point we are making:

Traditional Scheduling Approach	*Alternative Scheduling Approach*

1-Gantt Charts
  (for task management)
2-Milestone Charts
  (to monitor progress)
	1-Work Breakdown Structures
	  (to define and plan a project)
	2-Networking
	  (to further plan; to isolate the
	  critical path and manage to it)
	3-Resource Analysis & Leveling
	  (to establish the most efficient
	  utilization of resources)

Alternative Scheduling Approach
(continued)

4-Gantt Charts
  (for task management)
5-Milestone Charts
  (to monitor progress)

On the left is what might be called the traditional scheduling approach. This is probably the type of scheduling used by most firms today. And it is probably adequate for most firms today. It is simple, and everyone can perform his or her part in concert with the overall direction of the firm.

On the right is shown what we will call an alternative to the traditional scheduling approach. It calls for the use of a WBS to plan and define the work; for a network to isolate the critical path and then to manage the project by managing the critical path; for analyzing resources and leveling them to their most efficient point, both for efficiency and to prevent over-commitment; and finally for the use of the more traditional methods of Gantt and milestone charts. By taking this alternative the project can proceed with better assurances that the final objectives can be met, because the issues of accomplishment have been clearly laid out and understood. Resources which will be required have been screened to determine whether or not they are available to achieve the intended goals. And lastly, only those levels of funds which are absolutely necessary to accomplish the goals will be requested because those tasks which can be delayed without a negative impact to the project will be postponed until they are needed. In some cases (but certainly not all) the alternative to the traditional scheduling approach is the more appropriate one for a particular business to take.

Whether or not the art of scheduling has reached the point where it can now be considered a science is open for debate and there will likely be no absolute winners. The only message that we have been attempting to suggest is that the function of scheduling is vital for the optimum performance of any management. And further, that there is a full complement of scheduling techniques now available to all organizations, thanks particularly to the introduction of microcomputers and associated scheduling software. While some of the more sophisticated scheduling methods have been ignored in the past, for whatever practical reasons, successful managements in the future should examine all available tools for the appropriate application—or their competitors down the street will.

Glossary Of Scheduling Terms

Certain terms have been used in this book which are technical in nature and which are not likely to appear in most dictionaries. Therefore, the more common scheduling terms that we have used have been compiled and are listed below.

However, it should be recognized that there are professional differences of opinion (and expressions) even among the experts on the subject. Some experts will use a particular term in one way, with an emphasis on a special point, which may be slightly different than that used by others. In these cases and with certain terms which are particularly important to the subject, multiple definitions of the same term have been listed. The authors have not attempted to resolve these inconsistencies which exist between the quoted authorities. We present them here for your consideration.

ACTIVITY-Something that occurs over time. The subject of the plan, that which must be accomplished. Also referred to as a "Task."

ACTIVITY-An element of a project represented on a network by an arrow. An activity cannot be started until the event preceding it has occurred. An activity may represent: a process, a task, a procurement cycle, or waiting time. In addition, an activity may simply represent a connection or interdependency between two events on the network. (Author's note: This definition applies only to ADM networks.)

ALGORITHM-A set of logical steps that lead to a solution.

ALLOWANCE-A time increment included in the standard time for an operation to compensate the workman for production time lost due to fatigue and normally expected interruptions, such as personal and unavoidable delays. It is usually applied as a percentage of the normal or leveled time.

ARROW DIAGRAM-The early CPM term for a network.

ARROW DIAGRAM METHOD (ADM)-See also "Critical Path Method."

ARROW DIAGRAMMING METHOD (ADM)-A diagramming technique in which each activity is represented by an arrow connecting an I-node to a J-node. These nodes are commonly referred to as events, and are used to indicate the relationships between activities. (Also called activity-on-arrow or event-oriented technique.)

BACKWARD/FORWARD SCHEDULING-The two principal methods of scheduling are backward scheduling to meet a deadline and forward scheduling to produce as soon as possible. The former method is followed by starting with the required delivery date and calculating backward to determine the release date for the order. When several subassemblies with different lead times are involved, the scheduler must work backward along each subassembly line to set the lead times for component work orders. Forward scheduling is used most frequently for products that do not require assembly of components.

BACKWARD SCHEDULING-A scheduling technique where the schedule is computed starting with the due date for the order and working backward to determine the required start date. This can generate negative times, thereby identifying where time must be made up.

BAR CHART-A scheduling tool (also called a Gantt chart) that shows the time span of each activity as a horizontal line, the ends of which correspond to the start and finish of the activity as indicated by a date line at the bottom of the chart.

BAR (GANTT) CHART-The most common type of display, named for Henry Gantt, who first utilized this procedure in the early 1900s.

CAPACITY ANALYSIS-An analysis most frequently employed in a machine or process area to project capacity for additional business.

CONCURRENT or PARALLEL-Two or more tasks that are done at the same time or at times which overlap.

CONSTRAINT or DEPENDENCY or RESTRAINT-Things that cannot happen until something else happens first.

CONSTRAINT-Limitation or restriction on actions.

CONSTRAINT-A relationship of an event to a succeeding activity in which the activity may not start until the event preceding it has occurred. The term "constraint" is also used to indicate a relationship of an activity to a succeeding event in which the event cannot occur until all activities preceding it have been completed. A zero-time activity.

CPM-See "Critical Path Method."

CP/M-Control Program for Microcomputers. (Author's note: only included because of similarity to CPM in scheduling.)

CRASHING-Expediting a project activity.

CRASHING-The process of reducing an activity time by adding resources and hence usually cost.

CRITICAL-If delayed, it will delay the project.

CRITICAL PATH-A sequential path of activities through a network diagram from beginning to end of the project which has no total float. The total time required to transverse the critical path is the shortest time in which the project can be completed.

CRITICAL PATH-The longest path through the network in terms of the amount of time the entire project will take.

CRITICAL PATH-The longest path; the path that defines minimum project time; the path with the *least* total float; the path on which any activity expansion/delay lengthens the project duration.

CRITICAL PATH METHOD (CPM)-The methodology/management technique which makes analytical use of information regarding the critical path and other sequential paths through the network.

DEPENDENCY-See "Constraint."

DUMMY-Not real but shows precedence.

DUMMY ACTIVITY-An activity in a network diagram that requires no work, signifying a precedence condition only.

DUMMY ACTIVITY-This is a network activity which represents a constraint, i.e., the dependency of a successor event on a predecessor event, but which does not have activity time, manpower, budget, or other resources associated with it. A dummy activity is illustrated on the network by a broken line.

DUMMY ACTIVITY-Fictitious activities used to ensure that the proper activity relationships are depicted in the network.

EARLIEST FINISH-In a network diagram schedule, the earliest time an activity can be completed.

EARLIEST START-In a network diagram schedule, the earliest time an activity can be started.

EMPIRICAL-A statement or formula based upon experience or observation rather than on deduction or theory.

EVENT-Something that happens at a point or moment in time.

EVENT-A specific definable accomplishment in a project plan, recognizable at a particular instant in time.

EXTRAPOLATION-Estimating the future value of some data series based on past observations.

FLOAT-See also "Slack."

FLOAT-The measure of spare time on each job.

FLOAT-The difference between the computed time available in which a task may be completed and the estimated duration time assigned to the task.

FLOAT (CPM)-Total float is the spare time available when all preceding activities occur at the earliest possible times and all succeeding activities occur at the latest possible times. Free float is the spare time available when all preceding activities start at the earliest possible times and all succeeding activities occur at the earliest possible times. Independent float is the spare time available when all preceding activities occur at the latest possible times and all succeeding activities occur at the earliest possible times.

FLOW PROCESS CHART-A graphic representation of the sequence of all operations, transportations, inspections, delays, and shortages occurring during a process or procedure.

FORWARD PASS-The forward (left to right) computation of the earliest expected time or date for each event(TE) and/or activity (EEC) on the network, starting with the first event.

FORWARD SCHEDULING-A scheduling technique where the scheduler proceeds from a known start date and computes the completion date for an order usually from the first operation to the last.

FRAGNETS-Standardized network modules to describe a specific task or series of tasks, used repetitively as needed in the development of a network.

FRAGNETS-See also "Subnetwork."

FREE FLOAT-The time by which a job can be expanded or delayed without affecting a subsequent job.

FREE FLOAT-That float which will not affect any succeeding activities.

FREE FLOAT-The amount of time an activity can be delayed from its earliest start time to the point where it interferes with the earliest start time of its succeeding activity.

FREE SLACK-The amount of time an activity can slip and not delay the start of any subsequent activity.

GANTT CHART-A bar chart developed by Henry L. Gantt during World War I.

GANTT CHART-A chart with time along the horizontal axis used to display the status of multiple jobs, machines, and so on.

HAMMOCK ACTIVITY-Summary of a group or series of activities. Duration is based upon the start of the first event and the finish of the last event in a series of arrow activities.

HAMMOCKING-A technique for summarizing a detailed network. The resulting summary network contains all of the original logic, but with fewer events/activities being displayed.

IDC-In due course.

I J NETWORKS-See "Critical Path Method."

LATEST FINISH-In a network diagram schedule, the latest time an activity can be finished.

LATEST START-In a network diagram schedule, the latest time an activity can be started.

LEARNING CURVE-A quantitative technique used to predict resource requirements in a manufacturing operation. The primary application has been the prediction of the direct manufacturing hours required to produce a known quantity of a specific product.

LINE OF BALANCE-A technique for assembling, selecting, interpreting, and presenting in graphic form the essential factors involved in a production process from raw materials to completion of the end product, against a background of time. It is essentially a management-type tool, utilizing the principle of exception to show only the most important facts to the audience. It is a means of integrating the flow of materials and components into manufacture of end items in accordance with phased delivery requirements.

LOGIC NETWORK-A diagram that complements and supports the work breakdown structure (WBS). The elements of the WBS are described in terms of control and reporting capabilities. The logic network establishes and gives direction to the work packages and tasks. The critical path method is used to determine the basis for the milestone schedule plan. Networks are normally to be provided in a PERT format. Work packages are usually tasks of short duration.

LOT SIZING-Determining production lot size.

M-DAY CALENDAR-See "Manufacturing Calendar."

MANAGEMENT BY DEFAULT-The failure to make a decision is, in itself, ultimately a decision.

MANAGEMENT BY EXCEPTION-A system of identification and communication that signals the manager when his attention is needed, and conversely, remains silent when his attention is not required.

MANAGEMENT BY OBJECTIVES-A program designed to improve employee's motivation through having them participate in setting their own goals and letting them know in advance precisely how they will be evaluated.

MANUFACTURING CALENDAR-A calendar, used in inventory and production planning functions, which consequently numbers only the working days so that the component and work order scheduling may be done based on the actual number of work days available. Syn: M-day calendar.

MASTER PRODUCTION SCHEDULE-A statement of what the company expects to manufacture. It is the anticipated build schedule for those selected items assigned to the master schedule.

MASTER SCHEDULE-Interrelates all tasks on a common time scale.

MASTER SCHEDULE-A master schedule is compiled to show, first, the total time available for the entire job if it must be finished by a certain time and, second, how the various portions of the job are to be scheduled.

MILESTONE-An event of particular importance, i.e., a big event.

MILESTONE-A major event in a project that typically requires the customer to approve further work.

MILESTONE-A key or major event in a project based on planned work accomplishment rather than a fixed time interval. Milestones are used to provide positive reporting points for effective management control. Interfaces are normally considered milestones.

MURPHY'S LAW-What can go wrong, will go wrong.

NEGATIVE SLACK-A condition in which the earliest expected time or date (Te) for an event is later than the latest allowable time or date (Tl) for the event, or in which the earliest completion time or date (EEC) for an activity is later than the latest completion time or date (LAC) for an activity.

NESTING-See "Hammocking."

NETWORK-A flow diagram consisting of the tasks and events that must be accomplished to reach the project goals, indicating their planned sequences of completion, interdependencies, and interrelationships.

NETWORK DIAGRAM-A pictorial representation of the logic among activities.

NETWORK DIAGRAM-A scheduling tool displaying activities or events as arrows and nodes that show the logical precedence conditions between them.

NETWORK NESTING-See "Hammocking."

NINETY NINETY RULE OF PROJECT SCHEDULES-The first 90% of the task takes 90% percent of the time, the last 10% takes the other 90%.

NORMAL TIME-The time an average worker takes when performing normally.

PARKINSON'S LAW-Work expands so as to fill the time available for its completion.

PARALLEL-See "Concurrent."

PATH FLOAT-Same as "Float" or "Slack."

PERT-Program Evaluation and Review Technique.

PERT-Programs Eventually Resolve Themselves.

PETER PRINCIPLE-The principle enunciated by Laurence J. Peter and Raymond Hall that managers tend to be promoted until they reach their level of incompetence.

POSITIVE SLACK-The condition when the latest allowable time or date (TL) for an event is later than the expected time or date (T_E) for the event, or when the latest completion time or date (LAC) for an activity is later than the earliest completion time or date (EEC) for the activity.

PRECEDENCE-The order in which tasks must be completed.

PRECEDENCE DIAGRAMMING-A network diagramming technique for showing the relationships of activities in a project. In such a diagram a rectangular box symbolizes an activity.

PRECEDENCE DIAGRAMMING METHOD (PDM)-A diagramming technique that represents each activity by a node or box. Arrows connecting these boxes are used to indicate the relationships between activities. (Also called activity-on-node or activity-oriented techniques.)

PRIMARY SLACK-The difference between the earliest expected time or date, (Te) or EEC, and the latest allowable time or date, (T_L) or LAC for the event or activity, expressed in weeks.

PROCESS CHART-A graphic representation of events occurring during a series of actions or operations and of information pertaining to those operations.

PRODUCTION SCHEDULE-A plan which authorizes the factory to manufacture a certain quantity of a specific item.

Project Management Institute (PMI)-A nonprofit professional organization devoted to advancing the state of the art in project management.

QUEUE-Waiting time.

QUEUE TIME-The amount of time a job waits at a work center before setup or work is performed on the job. Queue time is one element of total manufacturing lead time.

RESTRAINT-See "Constraint."

RISK-That level of uncertainty at which a decision maker knows, at least, the possible results of an action and can attach subjective probabilities to them.

RISK MANAGEMENT-The manipulation of corporate risk factors in the interest of the corporate objectives.

ROLLING WAVE CONCEPT-The rolling wave concept

recognizes that the further you look into the future, the less definition some project tasks will have. This concept requires that managers plan their work in as much detail as they can, and then progressively refine the work plan as the start date approaches.

SAFETY TIME-The difference between the requirement date and the planned instock date is safety time.

SCHEDULE-A time plan of goals or targets which serve as the focal point for management actions.

SCHEDULE-A timetable for performing activities, utilizing resources, or allocating facilities.

SCHEDULE-A list of the time certain things are to happen; a timed plan for a project; a list of details.

SCHEDULING-The act of preparing and/or of implementing schedules.

SCHEDULING-Establishing the timing for performing a task.

SCHEDULING RULES-Basic rules that are spelled out ahead of time so that they can be used consistently in a scheduling system. Such rules usually specify the amount of calendar time to allow for a move and a queue, how load will be calculated, etc.

SECONDARY FLOAT-Similar to total float, except that it is calculated from an intermediate event rather than from the project end date.

SEQUENCING-Determining the best sequence for work orders.

SEQUENTIAL-Things that happen in a sequence, serial, series, one thing after another.

SIMULATION-An imitation of reality with a model.

SLACK-See also ''Float.''

SLACK-Unutilized.

SLACK-The difference between the time expected and the time allowed for an event or activity. There are three conditions of slack: negative, zero, and positive. If the expected time exceeds the allowed time, there is negative slack. If the allowed time exceeds the expected time and the expected time are equal, there is zero slack. The slack along a given path calculated from the terminal point of the path is the primary slack. Within the network, events may have scheduled or directed dates assigned to them. During the backward pass calculation, slack can be computed using these scheduled dates as well as using the terminal event. The slack computed using certain scheduled or directed dates in the body of the network is called secondary slack.

SLACK TIME-The amount of time on any path in a network diagram other than the critical path that is the difference between the time to a common node on the critical path and the other path.

STANDARD FRAGNETS or SUBNETS-A standardized subordinate network used to reflect a simple repetitive task.

STANDARD TIME-Normal time plus allowances.

STANDARD TIME-1. The time that should be needed to set up a given machine or assembly operation. 2. The time that should be required to run one part/assembly/end product through that operation.

STATEMENT OF WORK (SOW)-A description of a product or service to be procured under a contract; a statement of requirements.

SUBNETWORK or SUBNET-A subdivision of a major network. Interrelationships between subnetworks for consolidation or integration into the major network are maintained by common interface events.

SUMMARY NETWORK-A summarization of detailed networks. Normally, only milestone and interface events are plotted on summary networks.

TASK-See "Activity."

THROUGHPUT TIME-The amount of time to go through an operation.

TIME NOW-The current calendar date, used primarily when updating networks.

TIME STANDARD-The predetermined times allowed for the performance of a specific job. The standard will often consist of two parts, machine set up and actual running.

TOTAL FLOAT-The amount of time an activity can be delayed or expanded before it impacts the *project end date.*

TOTAL FLOAT-The time by which a job can be expanded or delayed without making the project late. If it is used up it may involve re-scheduling a subsequent job.

TRIPLE CONSTRAINT-A concept which views all projects as having three areas of performance: cost/schedule/technical.

VARIANCE-Deviation from standard.

WHAT-IF-ANALYSIS-The process of evaluating alternate strategies.

WORK BREAKDOWN STRUCTURE-A product oriented family tree composed of hardware, services, and data which completely defines the project/program.

WORK BREAKDOWN STRUCTURE-A family tree hierarchy of the products requiring work to be performed in accomplishing the end objective. Unlike a genealogical family tree, however, the products on the lower branches are produced earlier in time than those above. Products that result from work efforts may be hardware, services, and data.

WORK BREAKDOWN STRUCTURE-A family tree, usually product oriented, that organizes, defines, and graphically displays the hardware, software, services, and other work tasks necessary to accomplish the project objectives.

WORK BREAKDOWN STRUCTURE DICTIONARY-A publication that verbally describes the tasks of WBS elements in product-oriented terms, and relates each element to the direct cost charging practices of the program.

WORK BREAKDOWN STRUCTURE ELEMENT-A discrete portion of a work breakdown structure. A WBS element may be an identifiable product, a set of data, or a service.

ZERO SLACK-A condition when the latest allowable time or date (Tl) for an event is equal to the earliest expected time or date (Te) for an event or when the latest completion time or date (LAC) for an activity is equal to the earliest completion time or date (EEC).

Index

A

Activity, 85
Activity, defined, 5, 256
Adams, John, x
ADM, 75-77, 108-110, 256
Alice in Wonderland, 33
American Association of Cost Engineers (AACE), 234-235
Anderson, David R., 90, —, 179
Aquilano (see Chase and Aquilano)
Archibald, Russell D., 29
Arrow Diagram Method (see ADM) Artificial Intelligence, 238-239
Automated Scheduling, 221-239

B

Backward Scheduling, 186, 257
Bar Charts, 47-48, (see also Gantt Charts)
Baseline Schedule, 146, 159, 247-249
Boodman, David M., 173
Booz, Allen, and Hamilton, 74
Boucher, Thomas O., 76

C

Carroll, Lewis, 33
Carter, Jesse, ix
Charette, Winfred, 77
Chase and Aquilano, 4, 44, 223
Cheshire Cat, 33
Clark, Wallace, 57
Combination Charts, 49, 50, 66, 69
Communications, 6
Computers, 40, 42, 221-239

C (continued)

Concurrent, defined, 5
Constraint, 45, 87-93
Constraint, defined, 5
Converging, 96, 99
Cost/Schedule Control Systems Criteria (see C/SCSC) CPM (Critical Path Method), 75-77
Critical Path, 126-128, 147-149, 257-258
C/SCSC, 22, 23, 29

D

Deis, Paul, 178
Department of Defense, 16, 17
Department of Energy, 17-22, 23, 25
Dependency, defined, 5
Diverging, 96, 98
DOD (see Department of Defense)
DOE (see Department of Energy)
Dummy Activity, 50, 258
Dummy Constraint, 90, 92, 93
du Pont, E. I., 75

E

Earliest Times, 128-132
Eisenhower, Dwight D., 15, 33
Elsayed, Elsayed A., 76
Event, 85-86
Event, defined, 5

F

Factory Output Chart, 183
First Article Schedules, 189-192
Float, 145-146, 258-259

267

About The Authors

QUENTIN W. FLEMING is a manager of a program master planning department at Northrop Corporation's Aircraft Division, Hawthorne, California. He has been with that company since 1968, except for a five-year leave of absence when he received an appointment with the United States Government and became the American Peace Corps Director in Iran and Bahrain.

Other books by Mr. Fleming include: *Doing Business on the Arabian Peninsula*, published in 1981 by AMACOM Division of the American Management Associations, New York; and *Put Earned Value (C/SCSC) Into Your Management Control System*, by Publishing Horizons, Inc., Columbus, Ohio, 1983. He holds the degrees of BS and MA in Management and an LLB, and is a member of the Project Management Institute. He and his family live in Southern California.

JOHN W. BRONN has twenty-eight years of experience in financial administration, cost and schedule controls, project/production/management, and tool engineering. He is an internationally recognized authority on project management systems design and implementation. He is a senior consultant with Humphreys & Associates, Inc., and lectures in the project scheduling, C/SCSC, and performance measurement in a production environment seminars.

He is a member of the Project Management Institute, American Society of Tool and Manufacturing Engineers, and the American Management Association. He and his family live in Colorado.

GARY C. HUMPHREYS is the founder and Chief Executive Officer of Humphreys & Associates, Inc, international consultants to management, headquartered in Newport Beach, California. The personnel of H & A have taught over 150,000 students in their public and private seminars. They specialize in project scheduling, C/SCSC, manufacturing performance measurement, and construction management.

He is past chairperson of the National Security Industrial Association (NSIA), Management Systems Subcommittee. He holds the degrees of BS in management and an MBA. He and his family reside in Southern California.